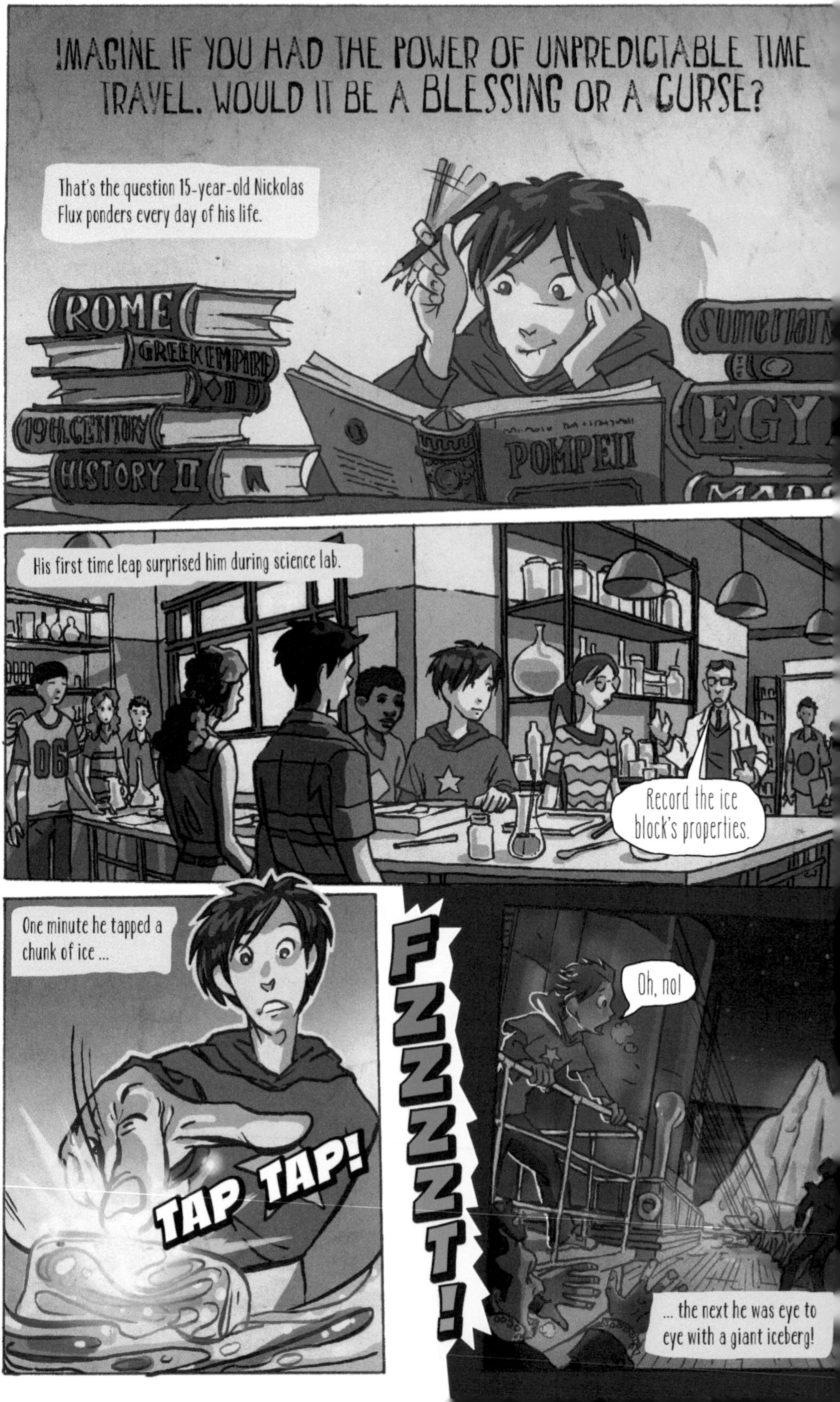
IMAGINE IF YOU HAD THE POWER OF UNPREDICTABLE TIME TRAVEL. WOULD IT BE A BLESSING OR A CURSE?
That's the question 15-year-old Nickolas Flux ponders every day of his life.
ROME
GREEK EMPIRE
19th CENTURY
HISTORY II
POMPEII
His first time leap surprised him during science lab.
06
Record the ice block's properties.
One minute he tapped a chunk of ice ...
TAP TAP!
FZZZZT!
Oh, no!
... the next he was eye to eye with a giant iceberg!

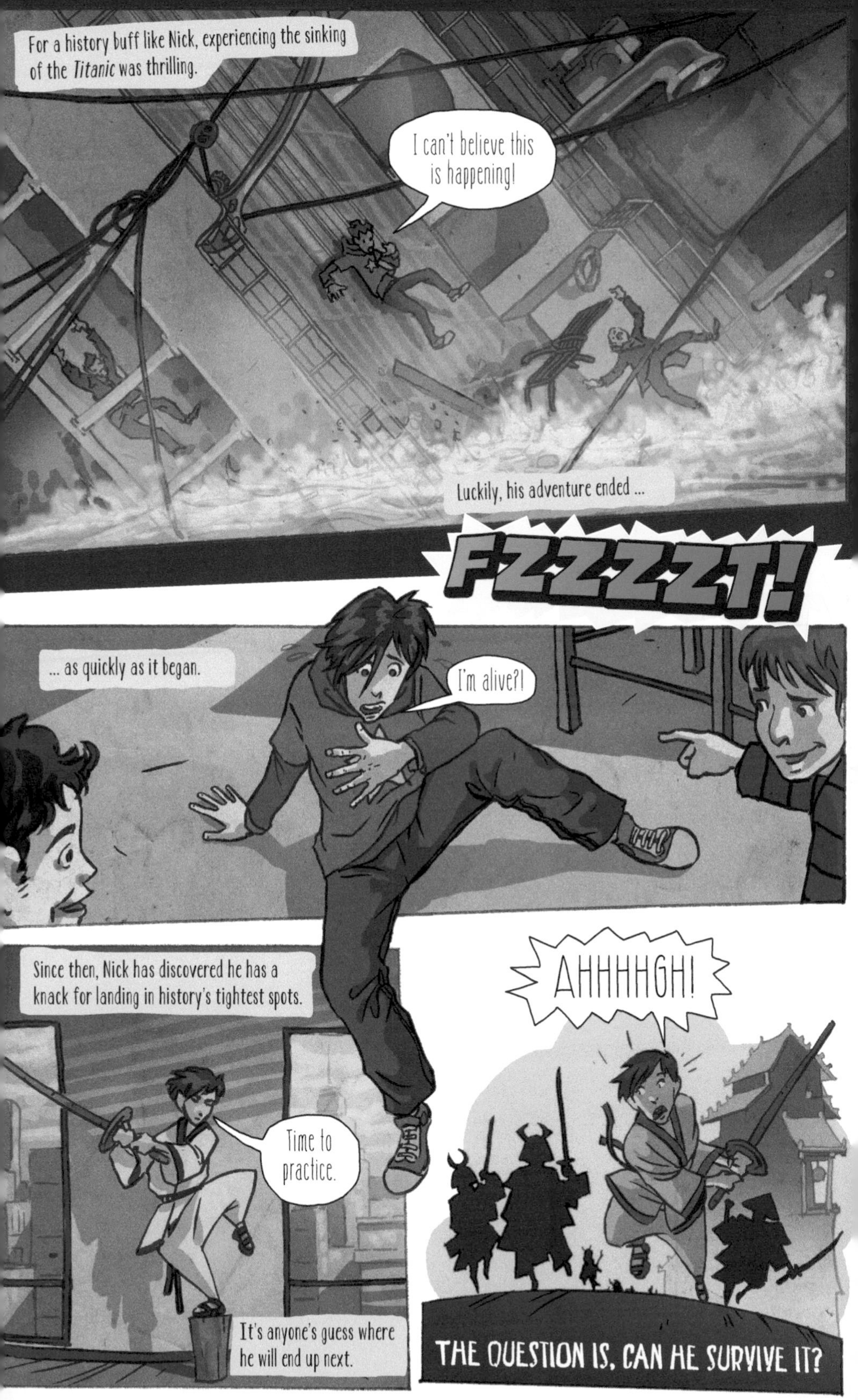
For a history buff like Nick, experiencing the sinking of the *Titanic* was thrilling.
I can't believe this is happening!
Luckily, his adventure ended ...
FZZZZT!
... as quickly as it began.
I'm alive?!
Since then, Nick has discovered he has a knack for landing in history's tightest spots.
Time to practice.
It's anyone's guess where he will end up next.
AHHHHGH!
THE QUESTION IS, CAN HE SURVIVE IT?

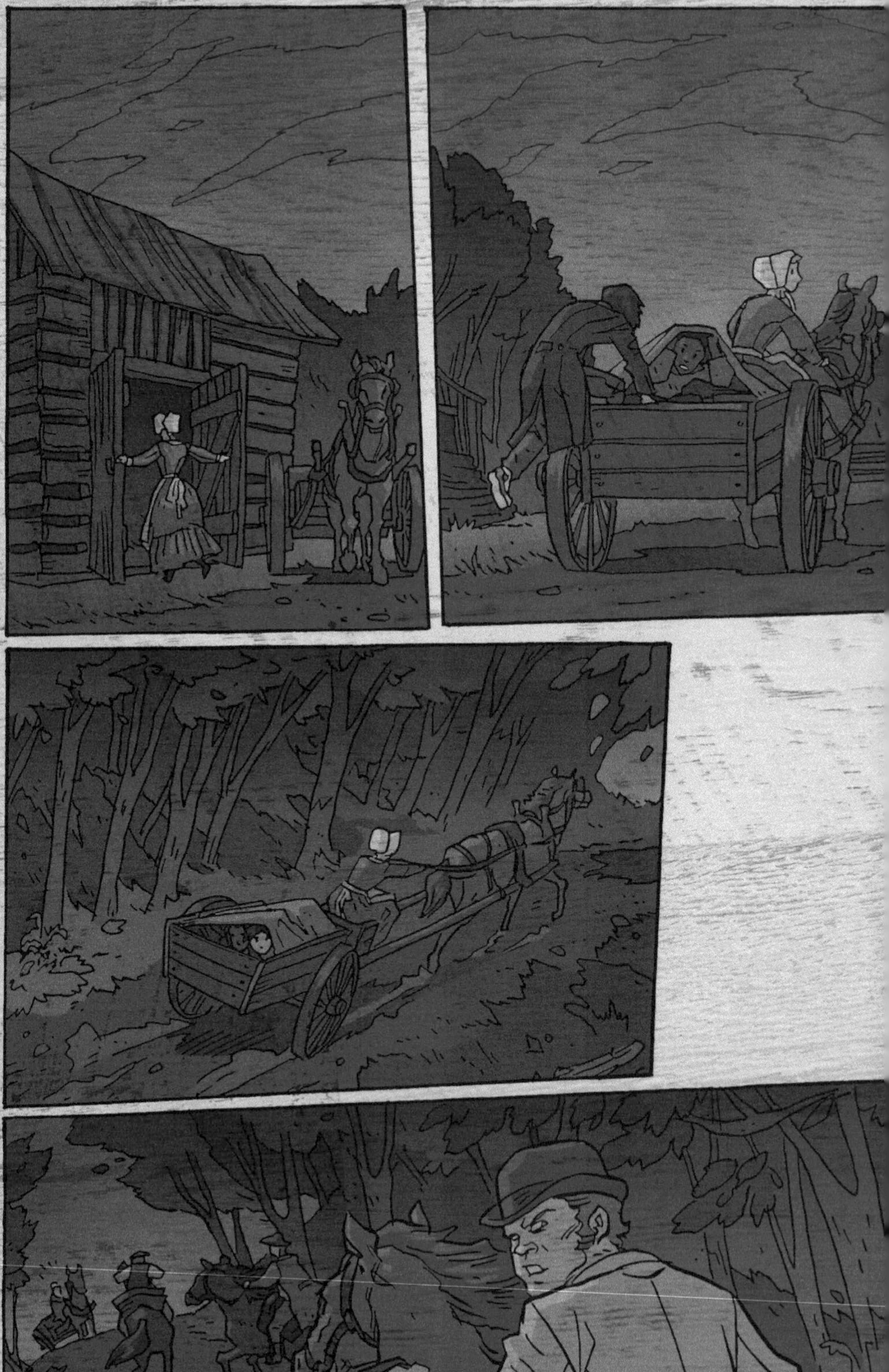

Nickolas Flux HISTORY CHRONICLES

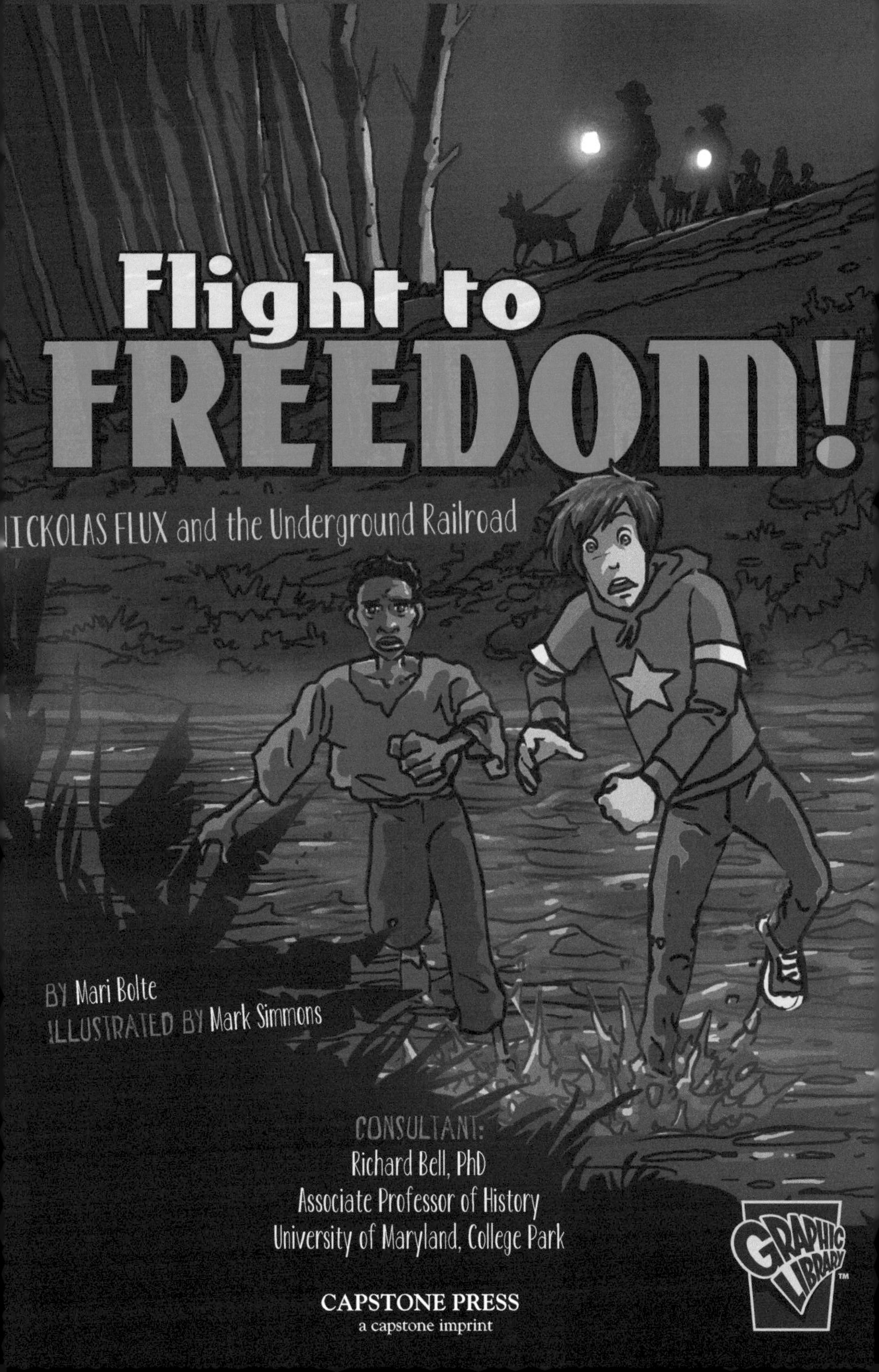

Flight to FREEDOM!

NICKOLAS FLUX and the Underground Railroad

BY Mari Bolte
ILLUSTRATED BY Mark Simmons

CONSULTANT:
Richard Bell, PhD
Associate Professor of History
University of Maryland, College Park

GRAPHIC LIBRARY™

CAPSTONE PRESS
a capstone imprint

Graphic Library is published by Capstone Press,
1710 Roe Crest Drive, North Mankato, Minnesota 56003
www.capstonepub.com

Library of Congress Cataloging-in-Publication Data
Bolte, Mari.
  Flight to freedom! : Nickolas Flux and the Underground Railroad / by
Mari Bolte ; illustrated by Mark Simmons.
    pages cm.—(Graphic library. Nickolas Flux history chronicles)
  Includes bibliographical references and index.
  Summary: "In graphic novel format, follows the adventures of Nickolas
Flux as he travels back in time and must survive a journey on the
Underground Railroad"—Provided by publisher.
  ISBN 978-1-4914-0254-2 (library binding)
  ISBN 978-1-4914-0259-7 (paperback)
  ISBN 978-1-4914-0263-4 (eBook PDF)
  1. Underground Railroad—Juvenile literature. 2. Underground
Railroad—Comic books, strips, etc. 3. Fugitive slaves—United
States—History—19th century—Juvenile literature. 4. Fugitive
slaves—United States—History—19th century—Comic books, strips,
etc. 5. Antislavery movements—United States—History—19th
century—Juvenile literature. 6. Antislavery movements—United
States—History—19th century—Comic books, strips, etc. 7. Graphic
novels. I. Simmons, Mark, illustrator. II. Title.
  E450.B68 2015
  973.7'115—dc 3   2014003772

Photo Credits:
Design Elements: Shutterstock (backgrounds)

EDITOR
Christopher L. Harbo

ART DIRECTOR
Nathan Gassman

DESIGNER
Ashlee Suker

PRODUCTION SPECIALIST
Jennifer Walker

COVER ARTIST
Dante Ginevra

Printed in the United States   5559

TABLE OF CONTENTS

INTRODUCING ...

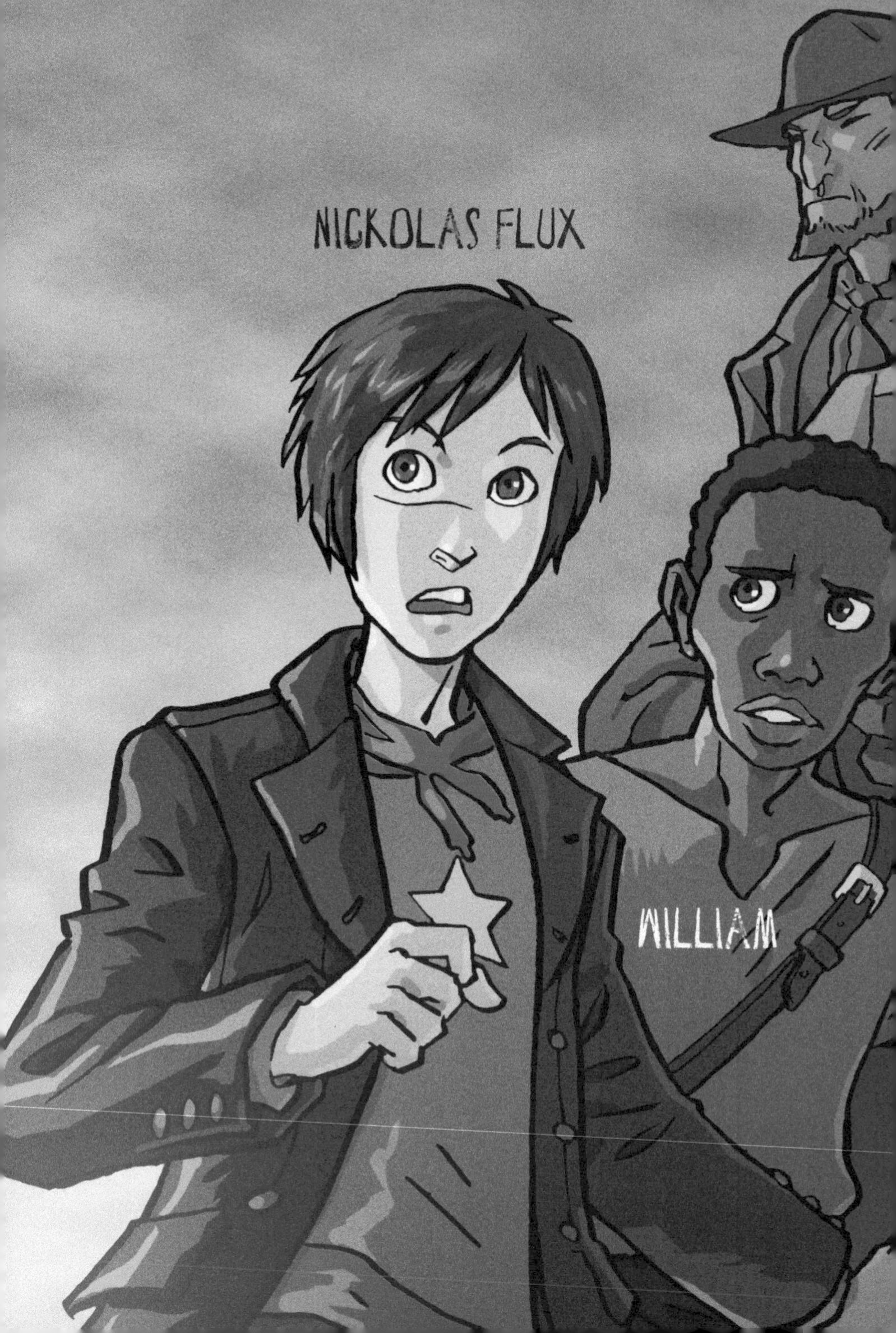
NICKOLAS FLUX
WILLIAM

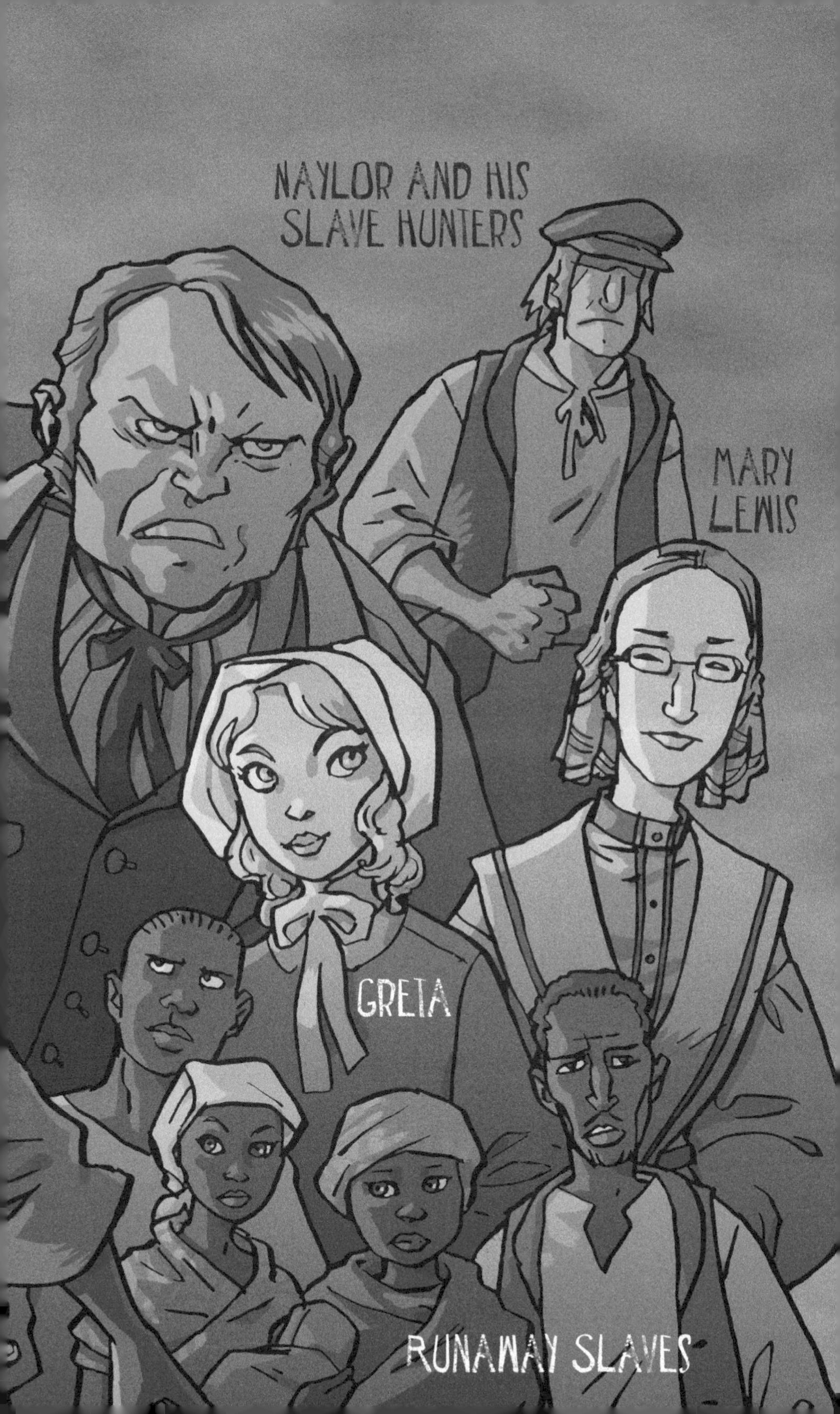
NAYLOR AND HIS SLAVE HUNTERS
MARY LEWIS
GRETA
RUNAWAY SLAVES

CHAPTER ONE

HANDS-ON HISTORY

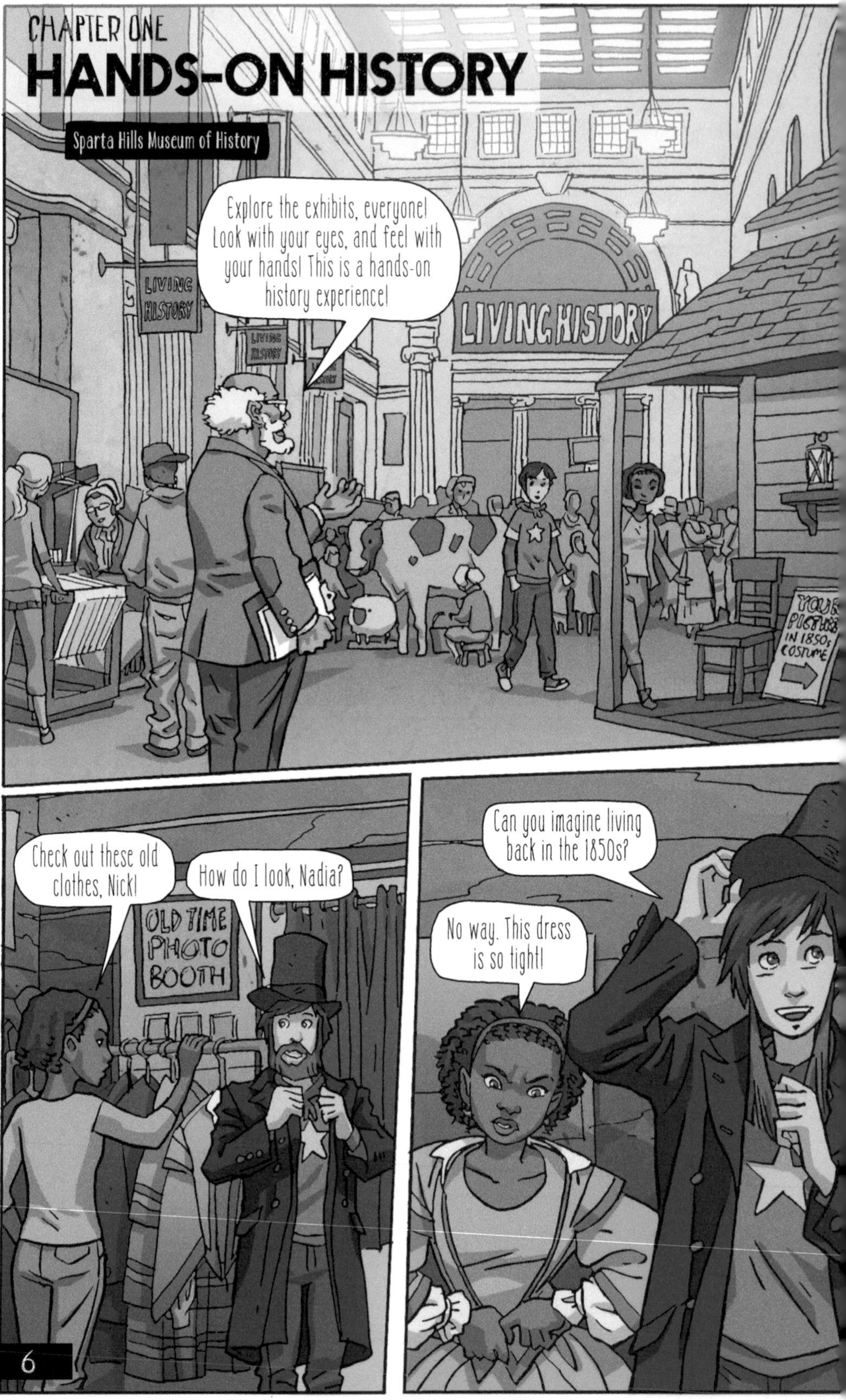

Sparta Hills Museum of History
LIVING HISTORY
Explore the exhibits, everyone! Look with your eyes, and feel with your hands! This is a hands-on history experience!
LIVING HISTORY
IN 1850s COSTUME
Check out these old clothes, Nick!
How do I look, Nadia?
OLD TIME PHOTO BOOTH
Can you imagine living back in the 1850s?
No way. This dress is so tight!

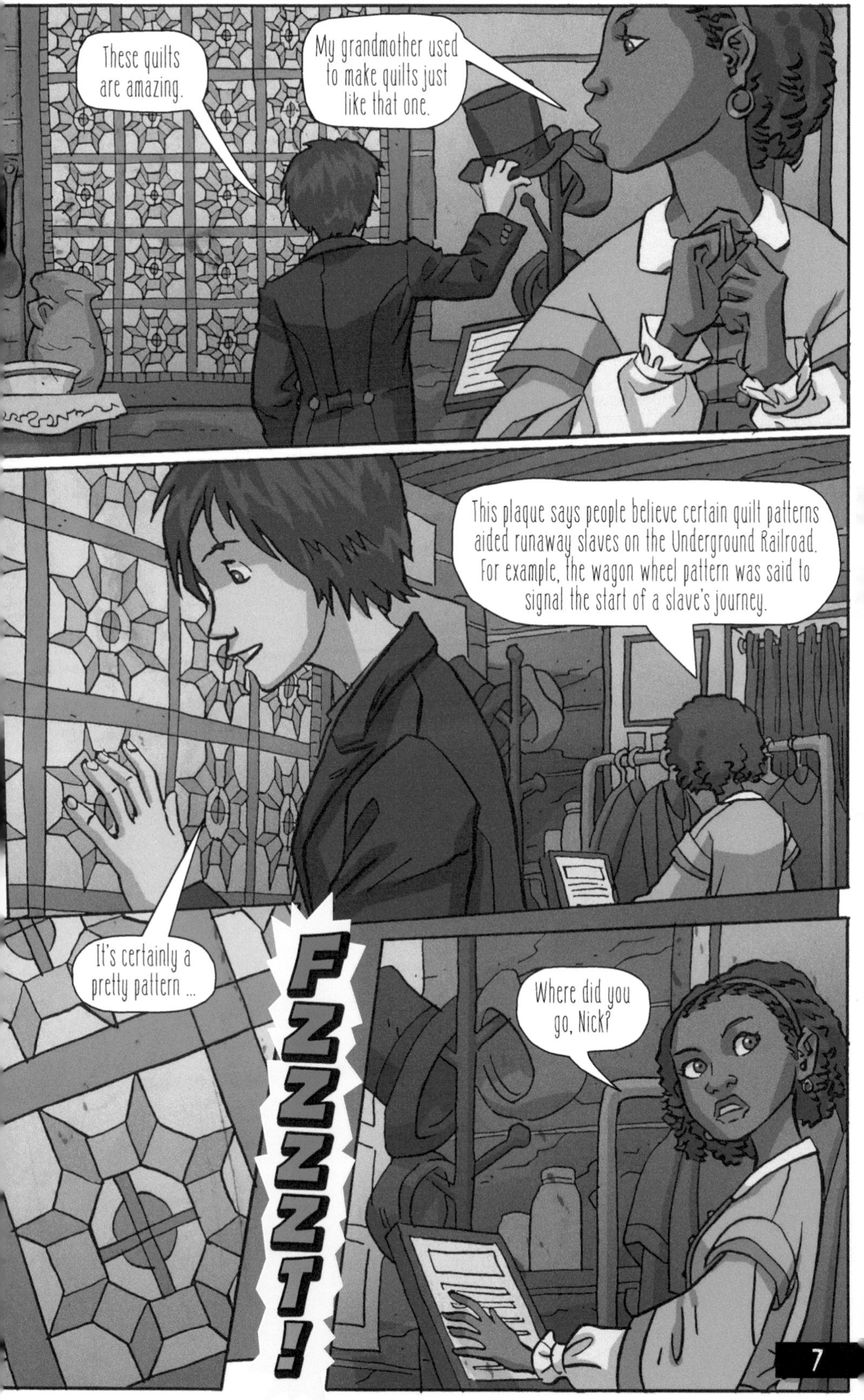
These quilts are amazing.
My grandmother used to make quilts just like that one.
This plaque says people believe certain quilt patterns aided runaway slaves on the Underground Railroad. For example, the wagon wheel pattern was said to signal the start of a slave's journey.
It's certainly a pretty pattern ...
FZZZZT!
Where did you go, Nick?

CHAPTER TWO

RUN FOR YOUR LIFE!

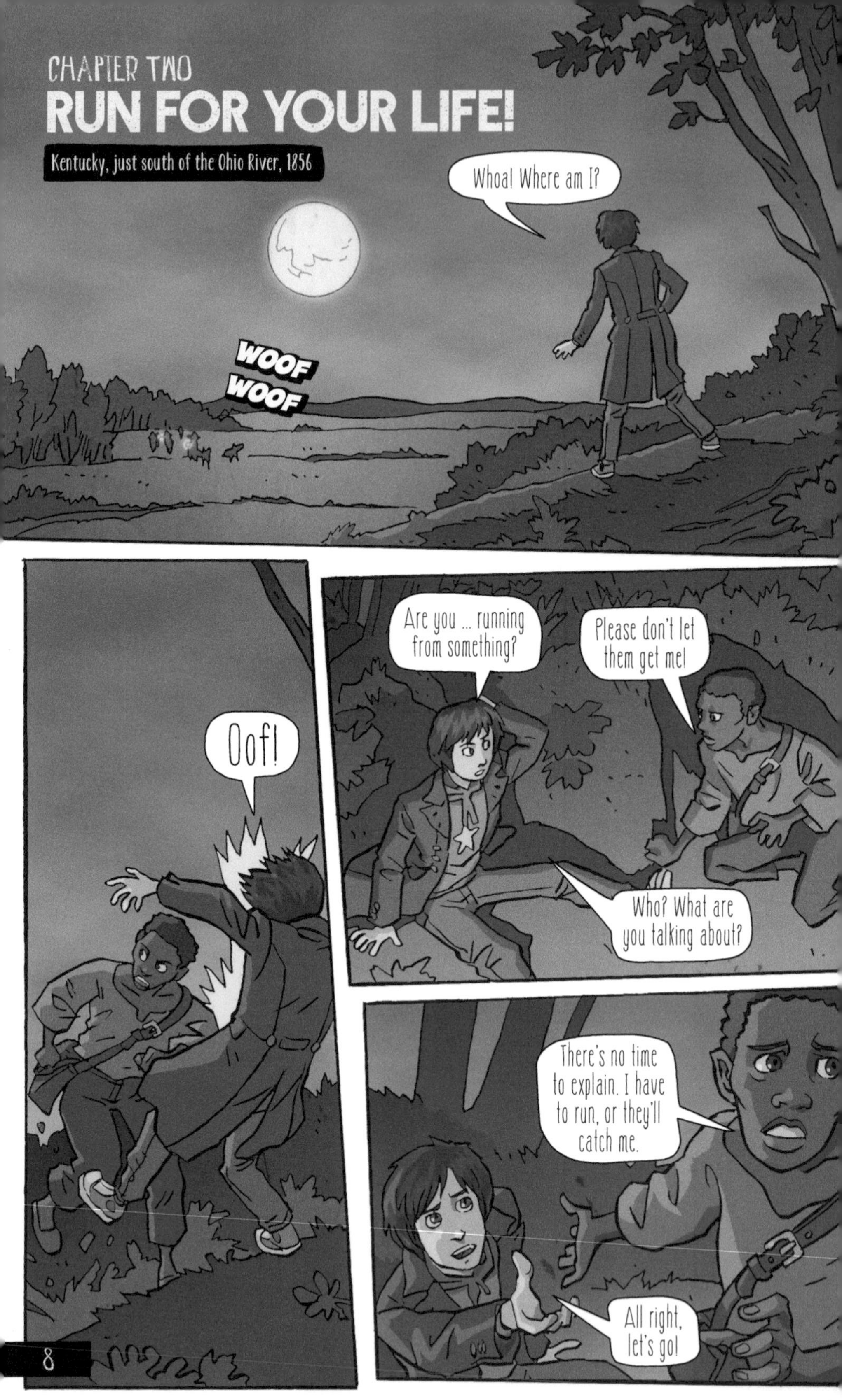
Kentucky, just south of the Ohio River, 1856
Whoa! Where am I?
WOOF
WOOF
Oof!
Are you ... running from something?
Please don't let them get me!
Who? What are you talking about?
There's no time to explain. I have to run, or they'll catch me.
All right, let's go!

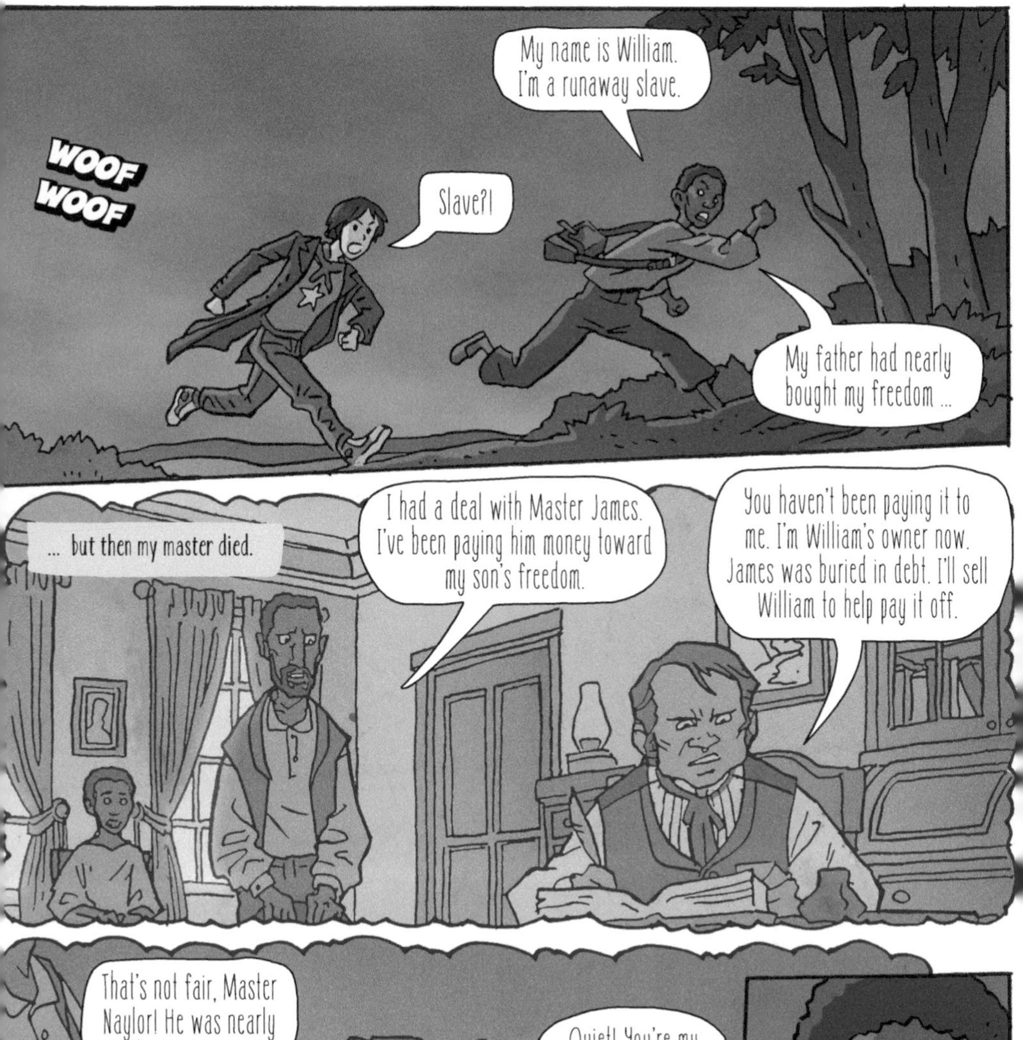
My name is William. I'm a runaway slave.
WOOF WOOF
Slave?!
My father had nearly bought my freedom ...
... but then my master died.
I had a deal with Master James. I've been paying him money toward my son's freedom.
You haven't been paying it to me. I'm William's owner now. James was buried in debt. I'll sell William to help pay it off.
That's not fair, Master Naylor! He was nearly done paying—!
Quiet! You're my property now. You'll speak when I let you.
That's when I decided to run away. I'm headed for Ohio, just across the river.

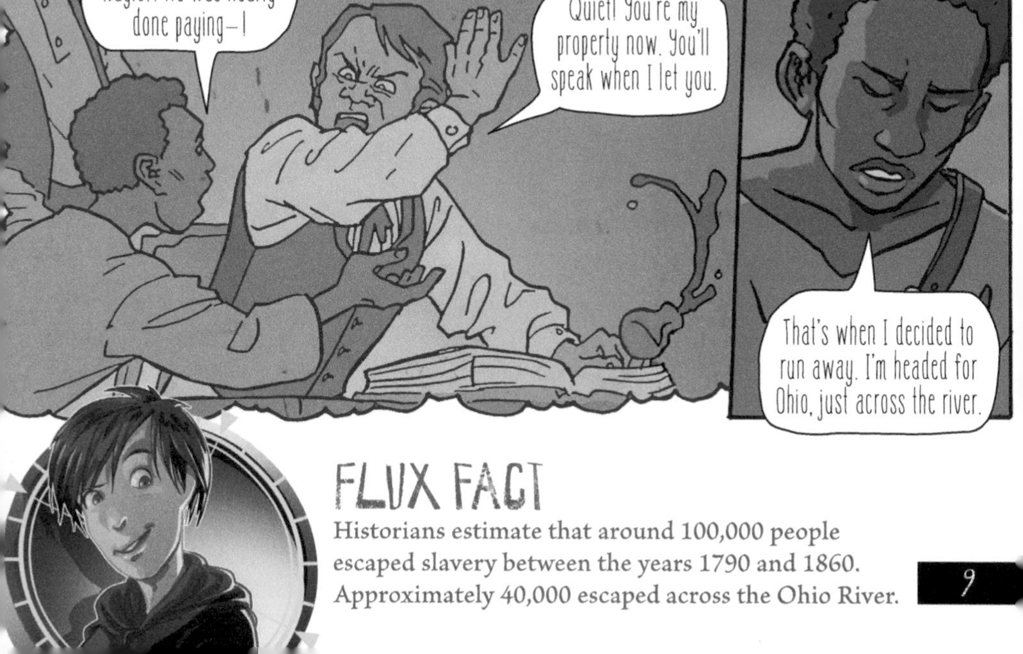

FLUX FACT

Historians estimate that around 100,000 people escaped slavery between the years 1790 and 1860. Approximately 40,000 escaped across the Ohio River.

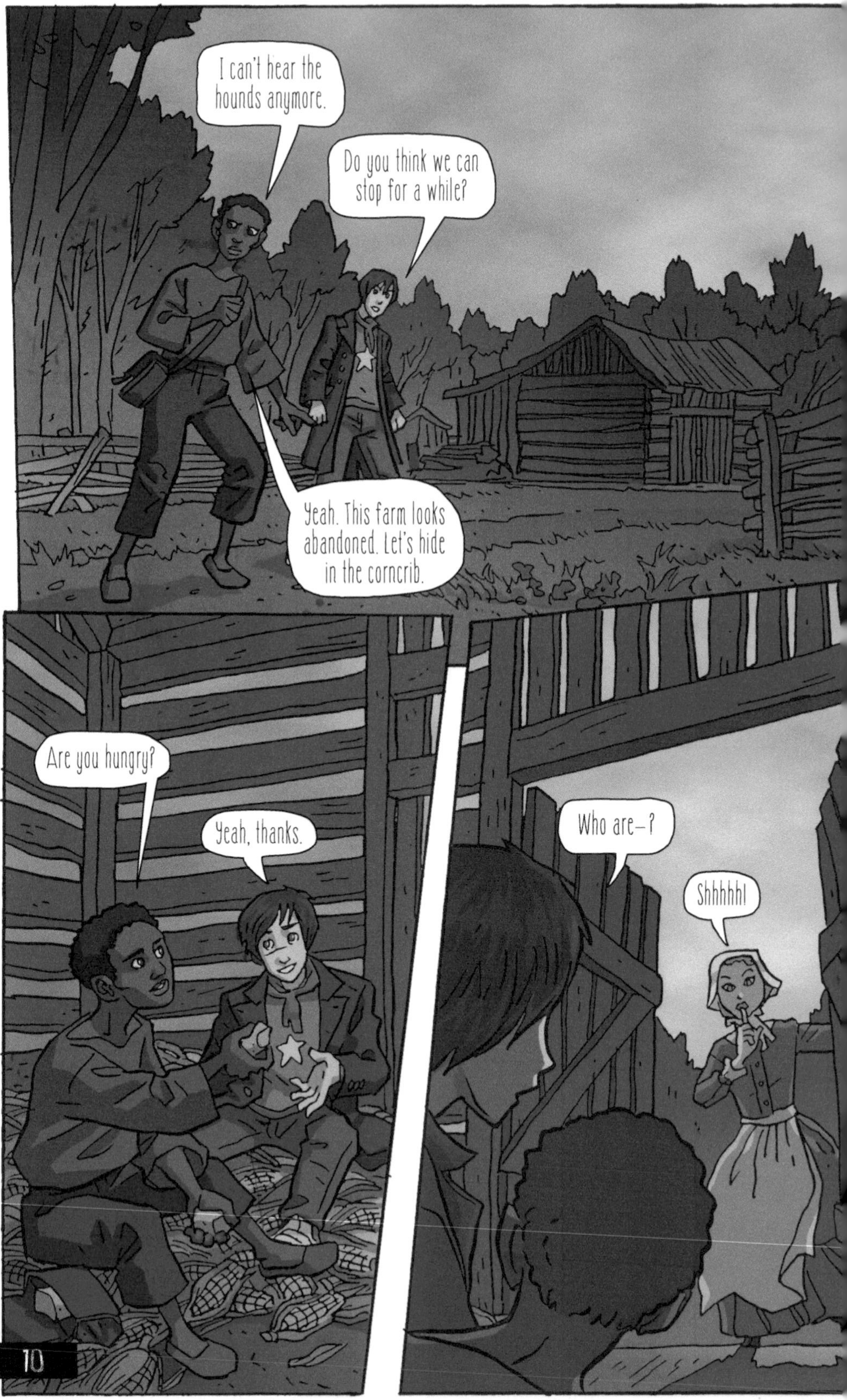

I can't hear the hounds anymore.
Do you think we can stop for a while?
Yeah. This farm looks abandoned. Let's hide in the corncrib.
Are you hungry?
Yeah, thanks.
Who are—?
Shhhhh!

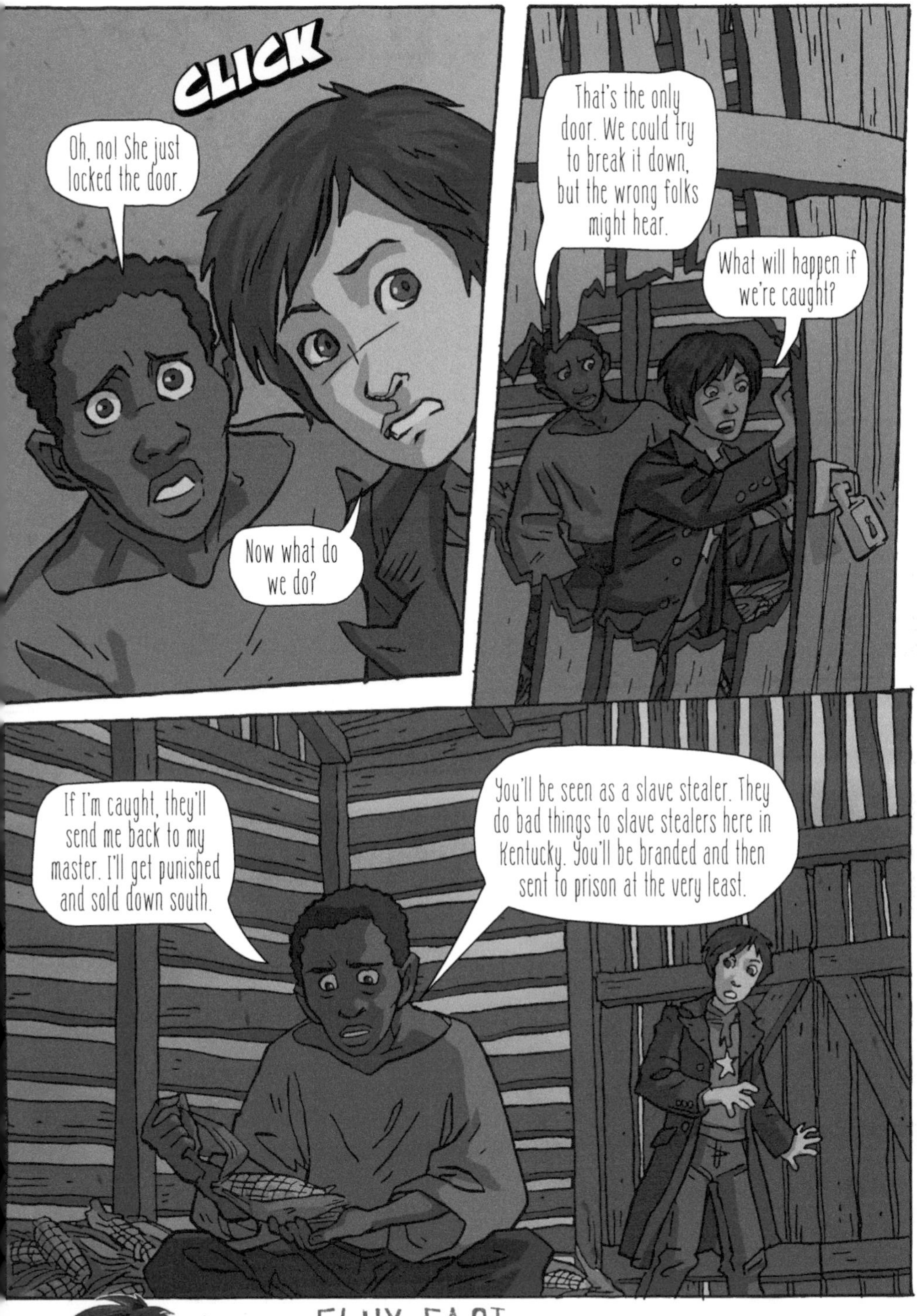
CLICK
Oh, no! She just locked the door.
Now what do we do?
That's the only door. We could try to break it down, but the wrong folks might hear.
What will happen if we're caught?
If I'm caught, they'll send me back to my master. I'll get punished and sold down south.
You'll be seen as a slave stealer. They do bad things to slave stealers here in Kentucky. You'll be branded and then sent to prison at the very least.

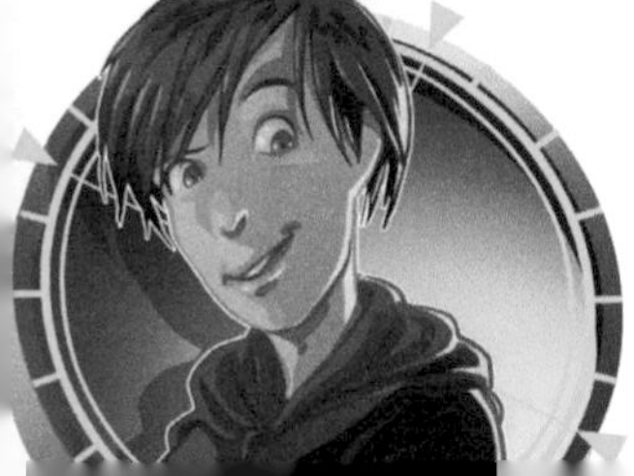

FLUX FACT

The Fugitive Slave Act of 1850 made it easier for slave owners to recapture runaway slaves. It required citizens in all states to detain runaway slaves. The act forced many runaway slaves to flee all the way to Canada to find true freedom.

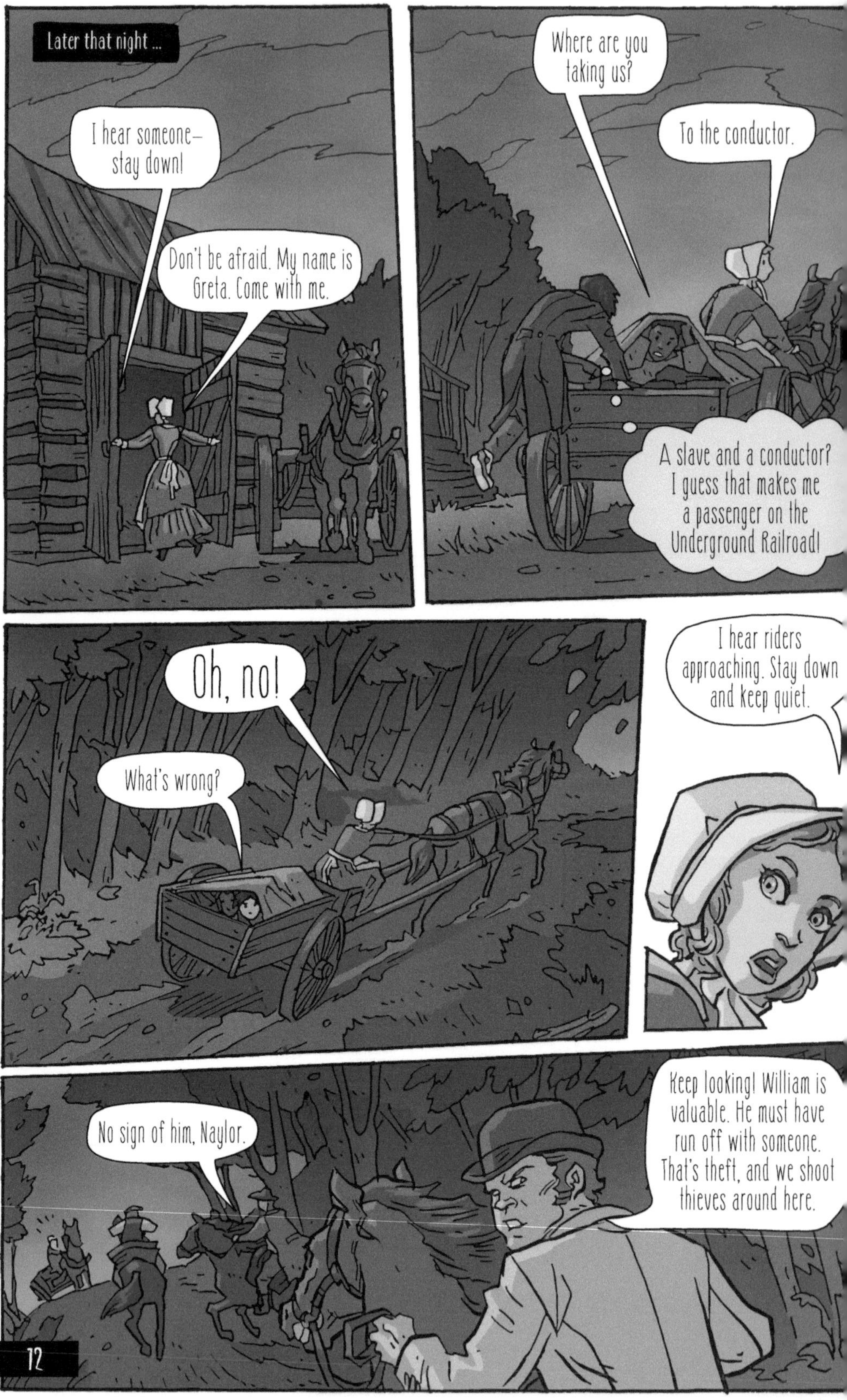
Later that night ...
I hear someone—stay down!
Don't be afraid. My name is Greta. Come with me.
Where are you taking us?
To the conductor.
A slave and a conductor? I guess that makes me a passenger on the Underground Railroad!
Oh, no!
What's wrong?
I hear riders approaching. Stay down and keep quiet.
No sign of him, Naylor.
Keep looking! William is valuable. He must have run off with someone. That's theft, and we shoot thieves around here.

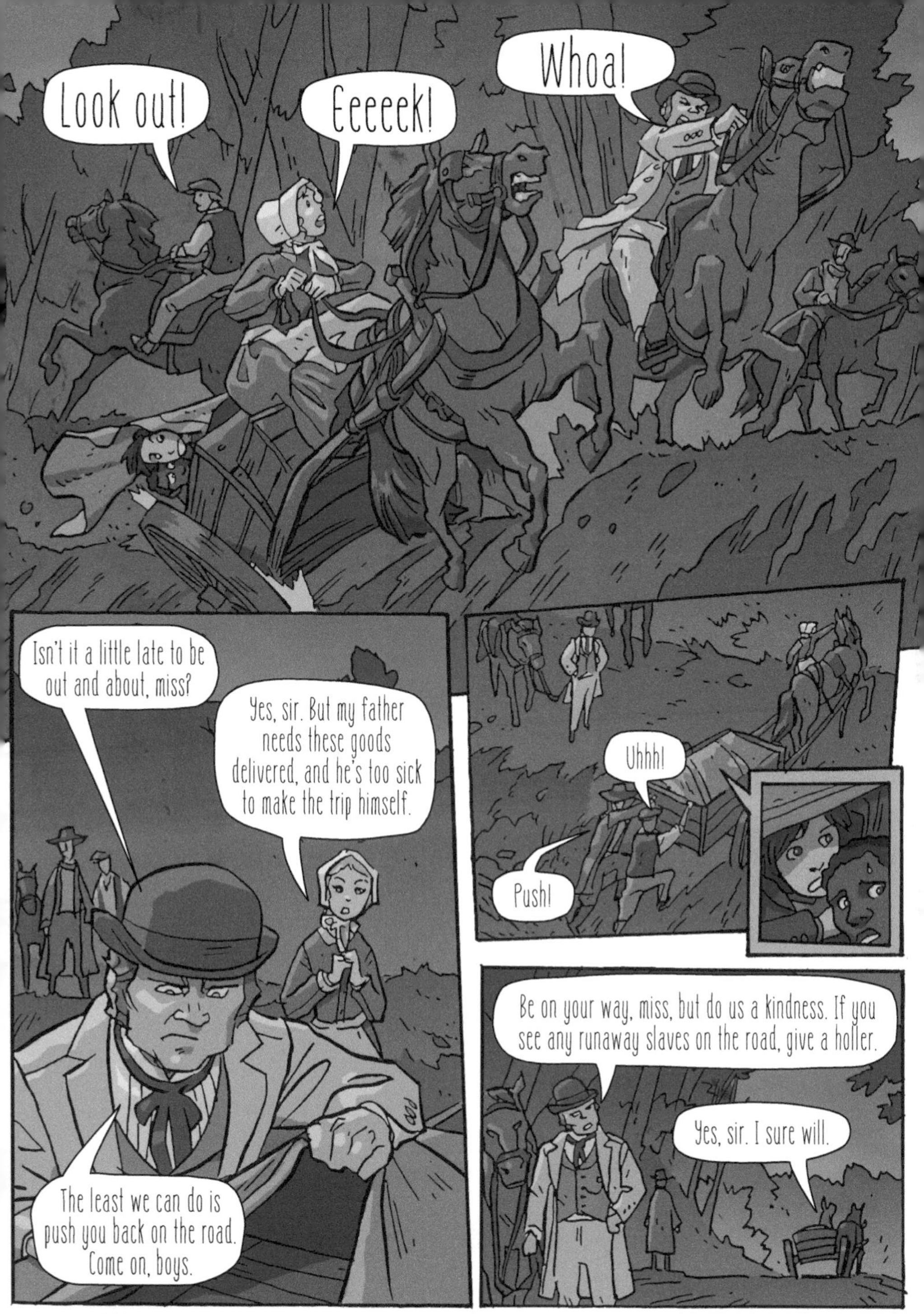
Look out!
Eeeeek!
Whoa!
Isn't it a little late to be out and about, miss?
Yes, sir. But my father needs these goods delivered, and he's too sick to make the trip himself.
The least we can do is push you back on the road. Come on, boys.
Uhhh!
Push!
Be on your way, miss, but do us a kindness. If you see any runaway slaves on the road, give a holler.
Yes, sir. I sure will.

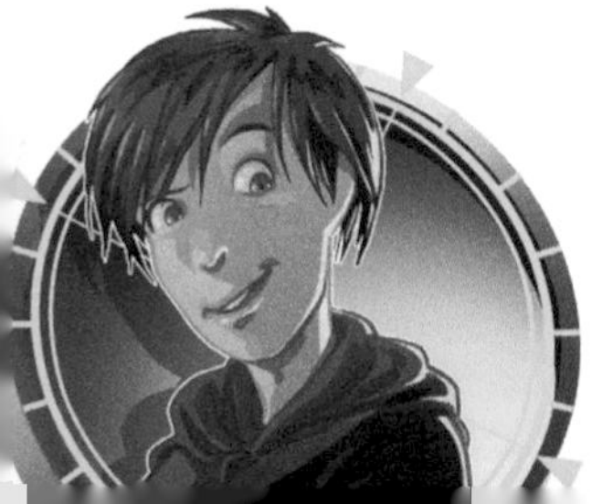

FLUX FACT

Kentucky was the last slave state runaways passed through before entering the North. About 300 slaves escaped through Kentucky to Ohio every year during the height of the Underground Railroad.

CHAPTER THREE

THE FIRST STATION

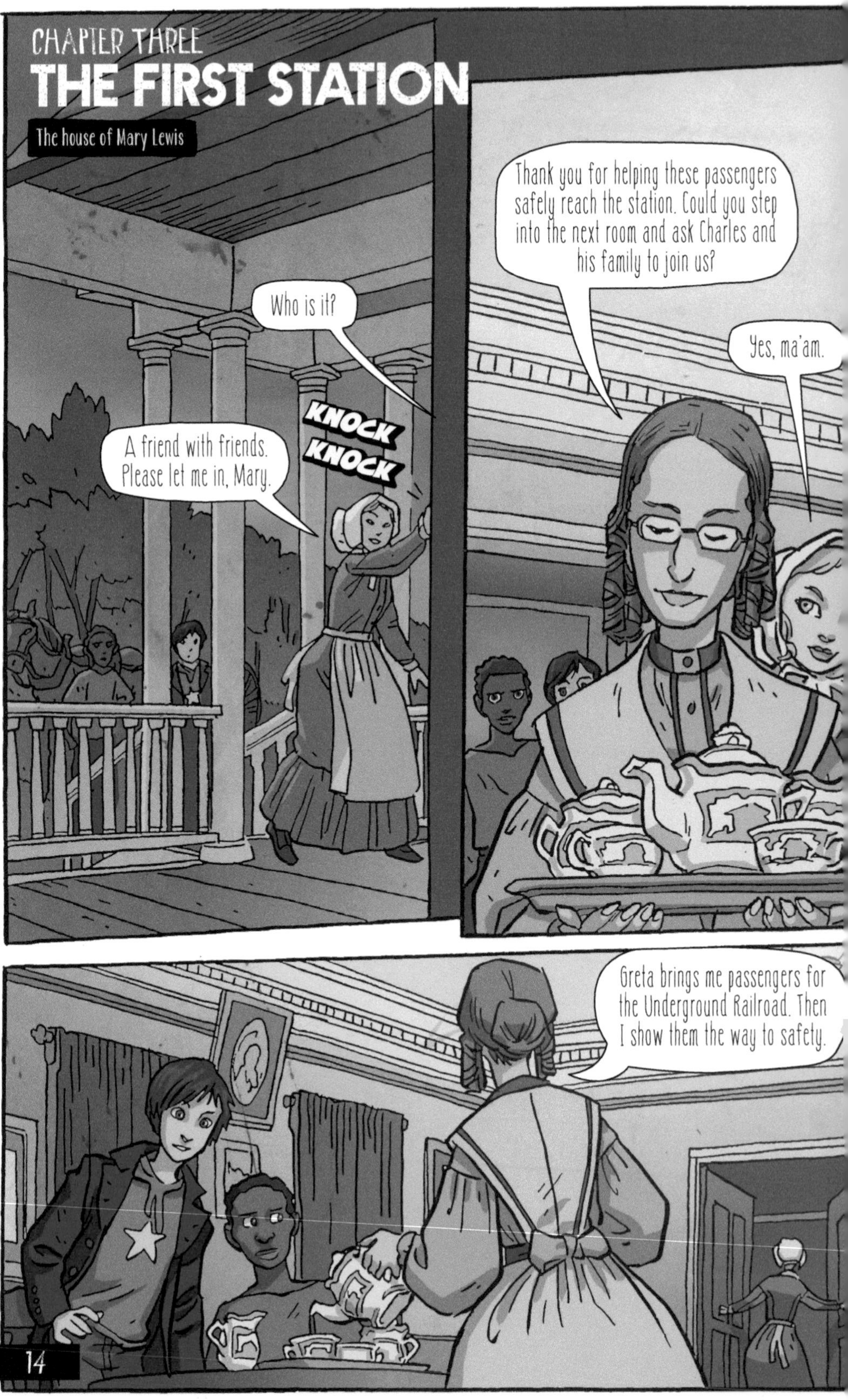
The house of Mary Lewis
KNOCK
KNOCK
Who is it?
A friend with friends. Please let me in, Mary.
Thank you for helping these passengers safely reach the station. Could you step into the next room and ask Charles and his family to join us?
Yes, ma'am.
Greta brings me passengers for the Underground Railroad. Then I show them the way to safety.

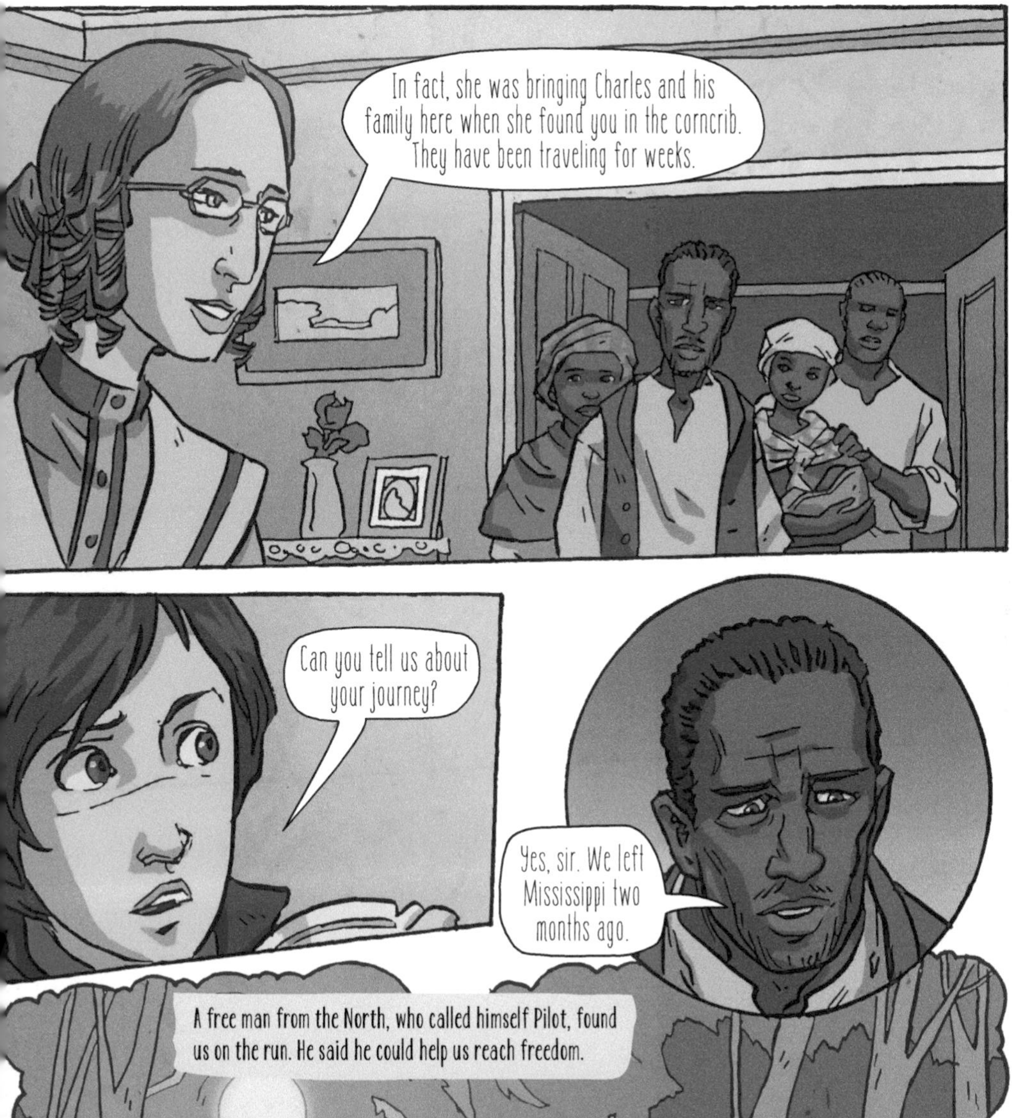
In fact, she was bringing Charles and his family here when she found you in the corncrib. They have been traveling for weeks.
Can you tell us about your journey?
Yes, sir. We left Mississippi two months ago.
A free man from the North, who called himself Pilot, found us on the run. He said he could help us reach freedom.

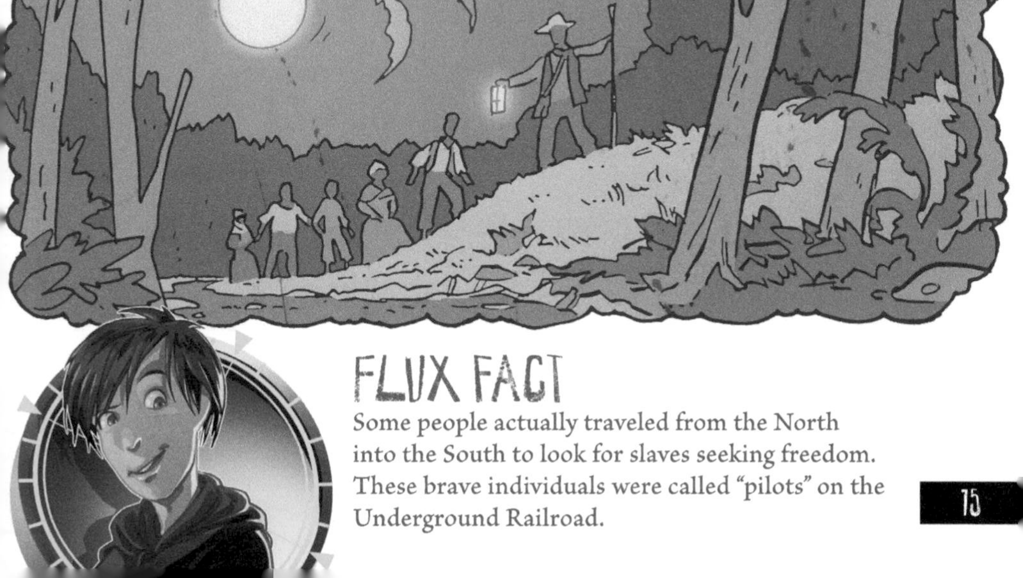

FLUX FACT

Some people actually traveled from the North into the South to look for slaves seeking freedom. These brave individuals were called "pilots" on the Underground Railroad.

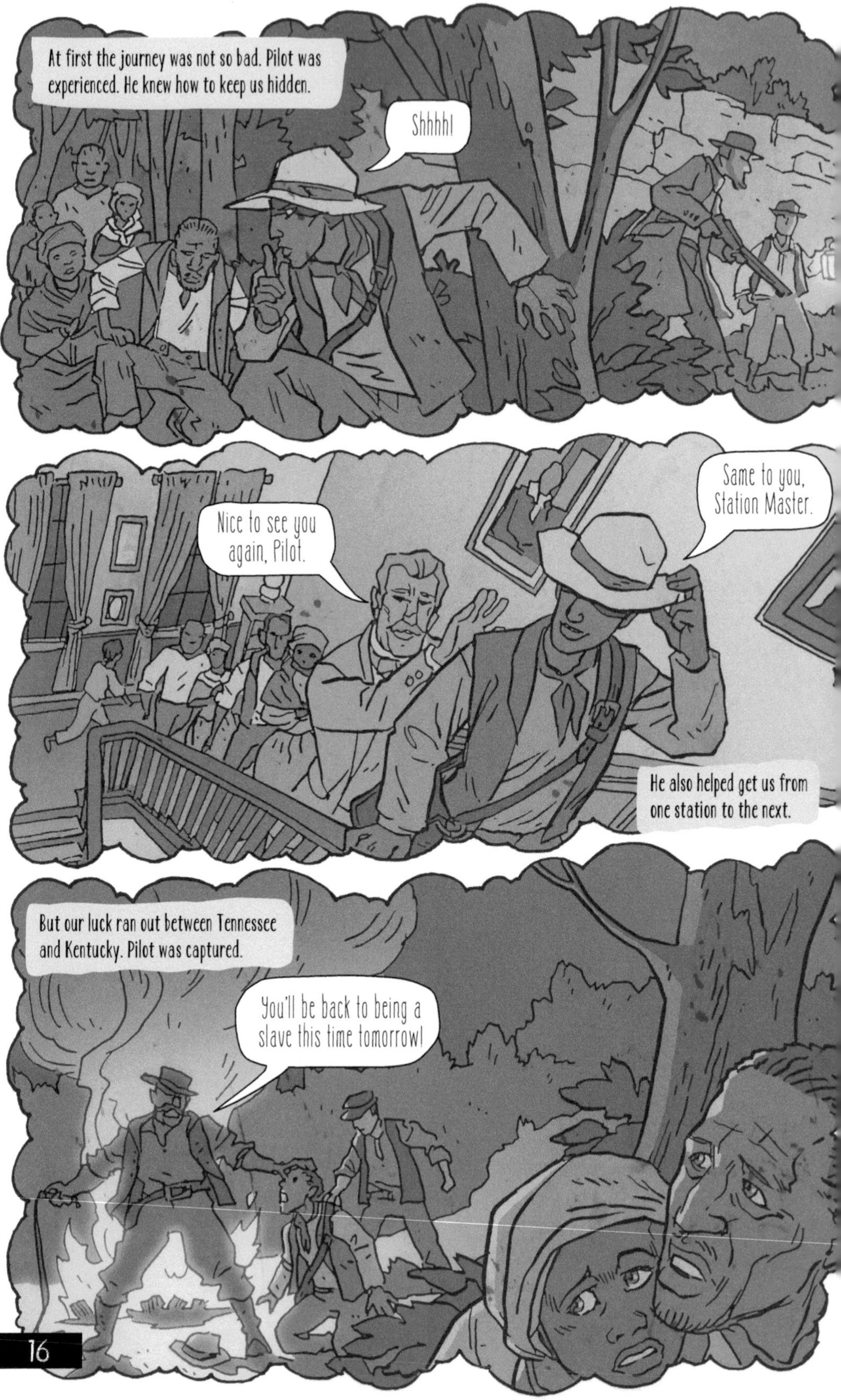

At first the journey was not so bad. Pilot was experienced. He knew how to keep us hidden.
Shhhh!
Nice to see you again, Pilot.
Same to you, Station Master.
He also helped get us from one station to the next.
But our luck ran out between Tennessee and Kentucky. Pilot was captured.
You'll be back to being a slave this time tomorrow!

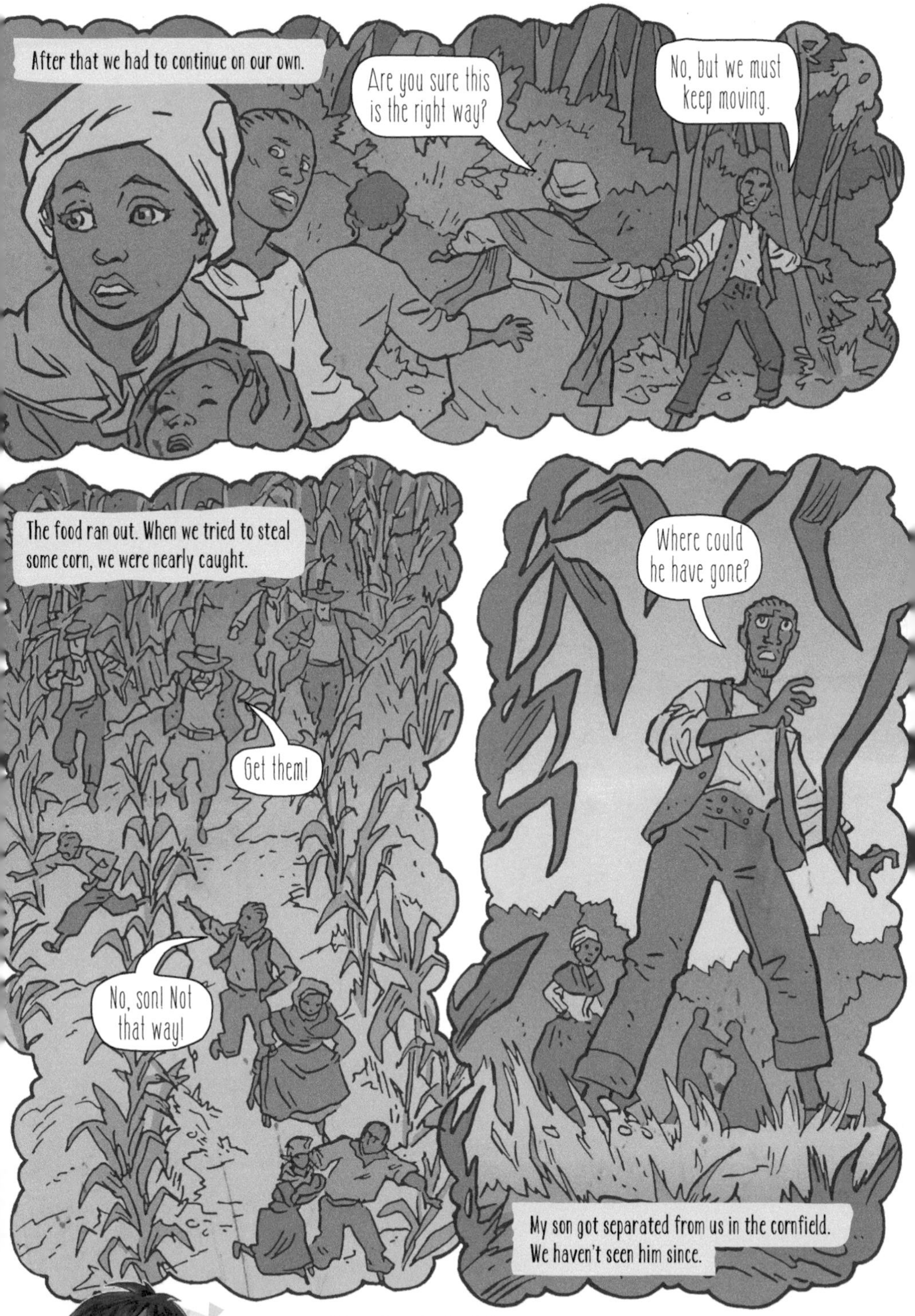
After that we had to continue on our own.
Are you sure this is the right way?
No, but we must keep moving.
The food ran out. When we tried to steal some corn, we were nearly caught.
Get them!
No, son! Not that way!
Where could he have gone?
My son got separated from us in the cornfield. We haven't seen him since.

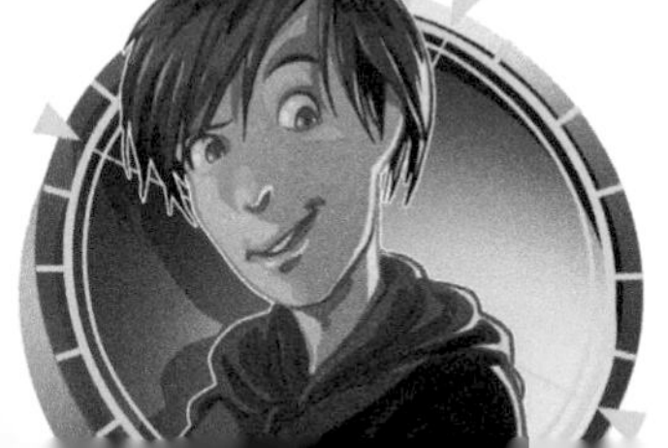

FLUX FACT

The Underground Railroad ran both ways. Bounty hunters and kidnappers captured free blacks and runaway slaves in the North. They took them to the South and sold them back into slavery.

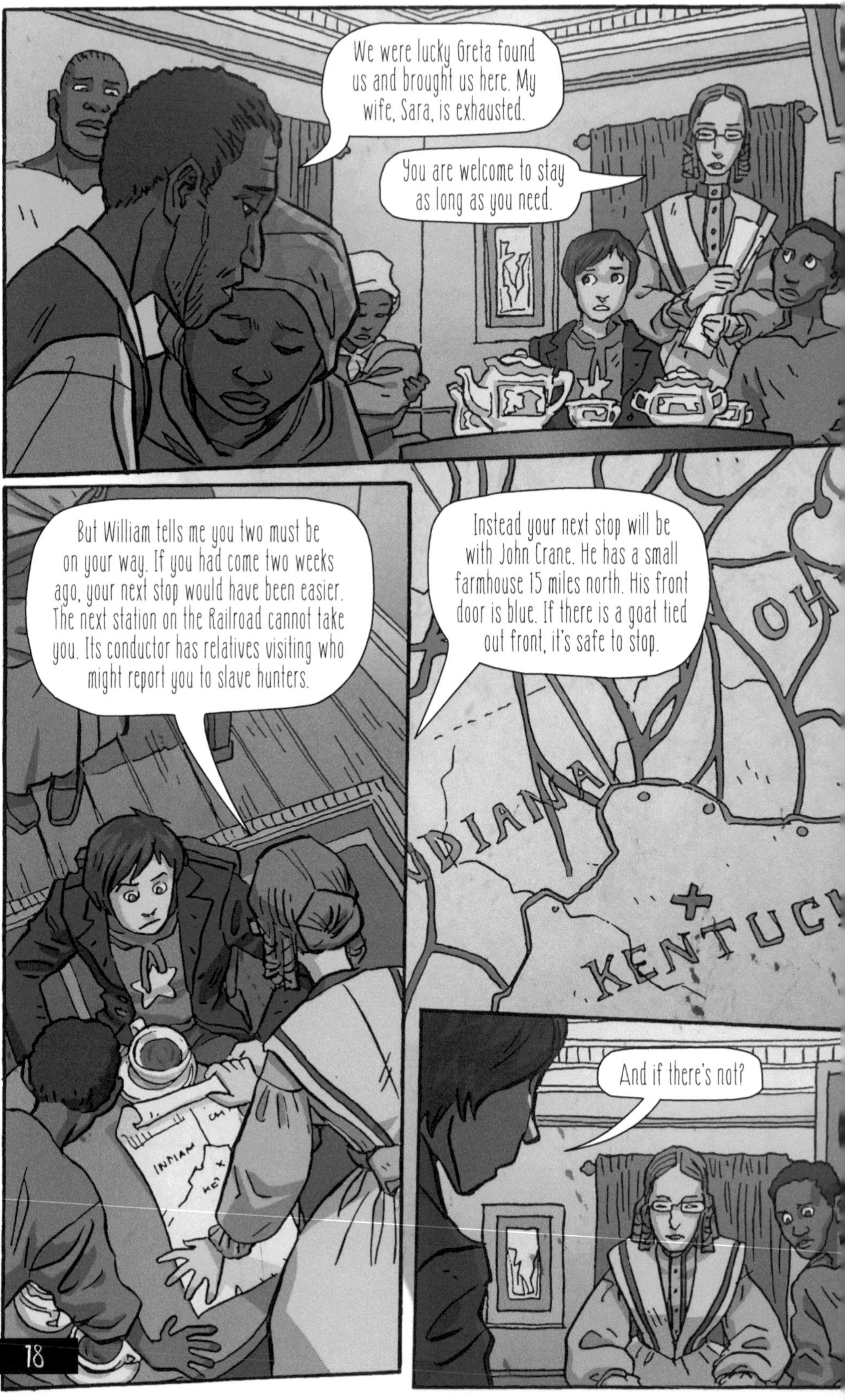
We were lucky Greta found us and brought us here. My wife, Sara, is exhausted.
You are welcome to stay as long as you need.
But William tells me you two must be on your way. If you had come two weeks ago, your next stop would have been easier. The next station on the Railroad cannot take you. Its conductor has relatives visiting who might report you to slave hunters.
Instead your next stop will be with John Crane. He has a small farmhouse 15 miles north. His front door is blue. If there is a goat tied out front, it's safe to stop.
OH
DIANA
KENTUC
And if there's not?

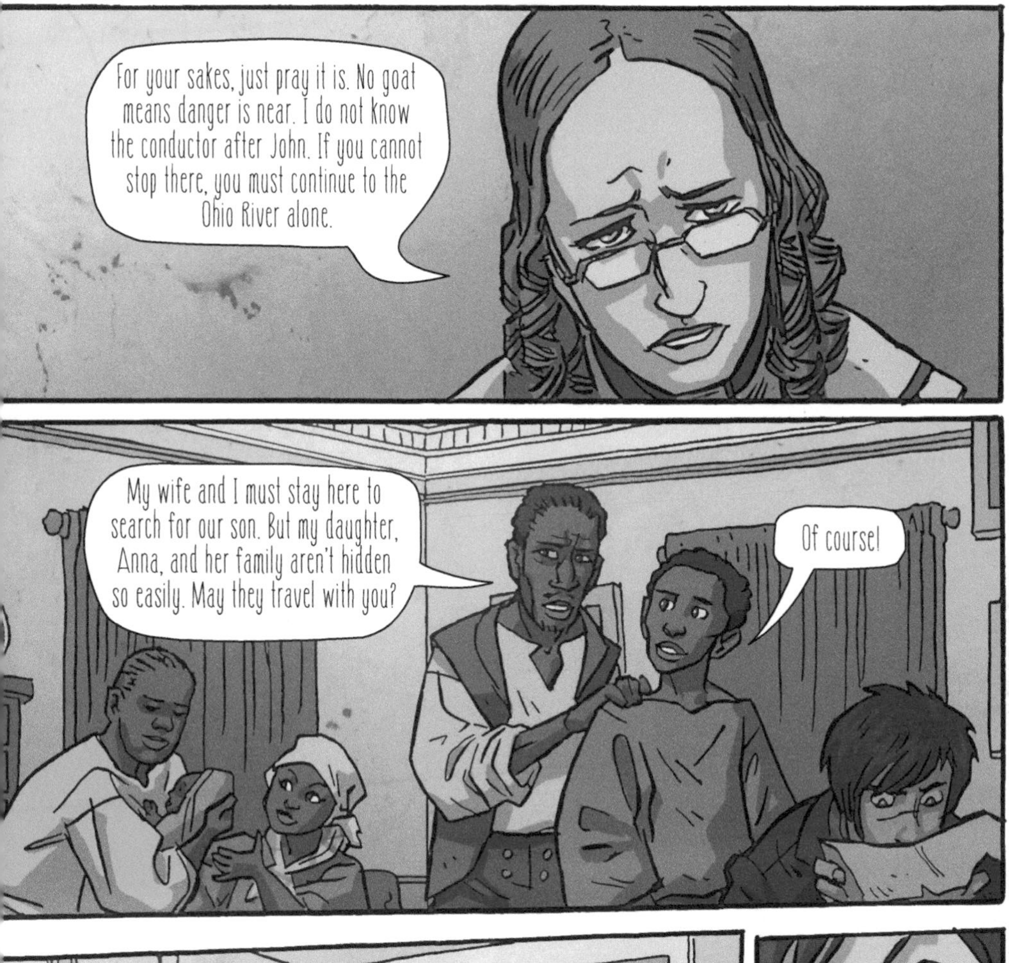
For your sakes, just pray it is. No goat means danger is near. I do not know the conductor after John. If you cannot stop there, you must continue to the Ohio River alone.
My wife and I must stay here to search for our son. But my daughter, Anna, and her family aren't hidden so easily. May they travel with you?
Of course!
May this pin bring you luck on your journey.
Thank you for everything, Mary.

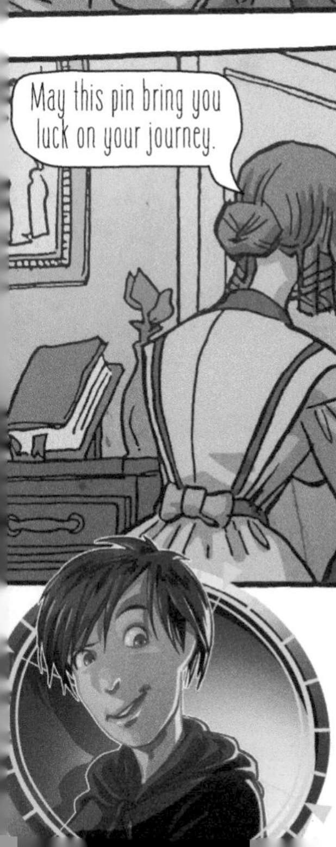

FLUX FACT

Conductors on the Underground Railroad faced great personal risk. They could lose their money, their homes, and even their lives. For their own safety, few records were kept. Some conductors used fake names and secret identities.

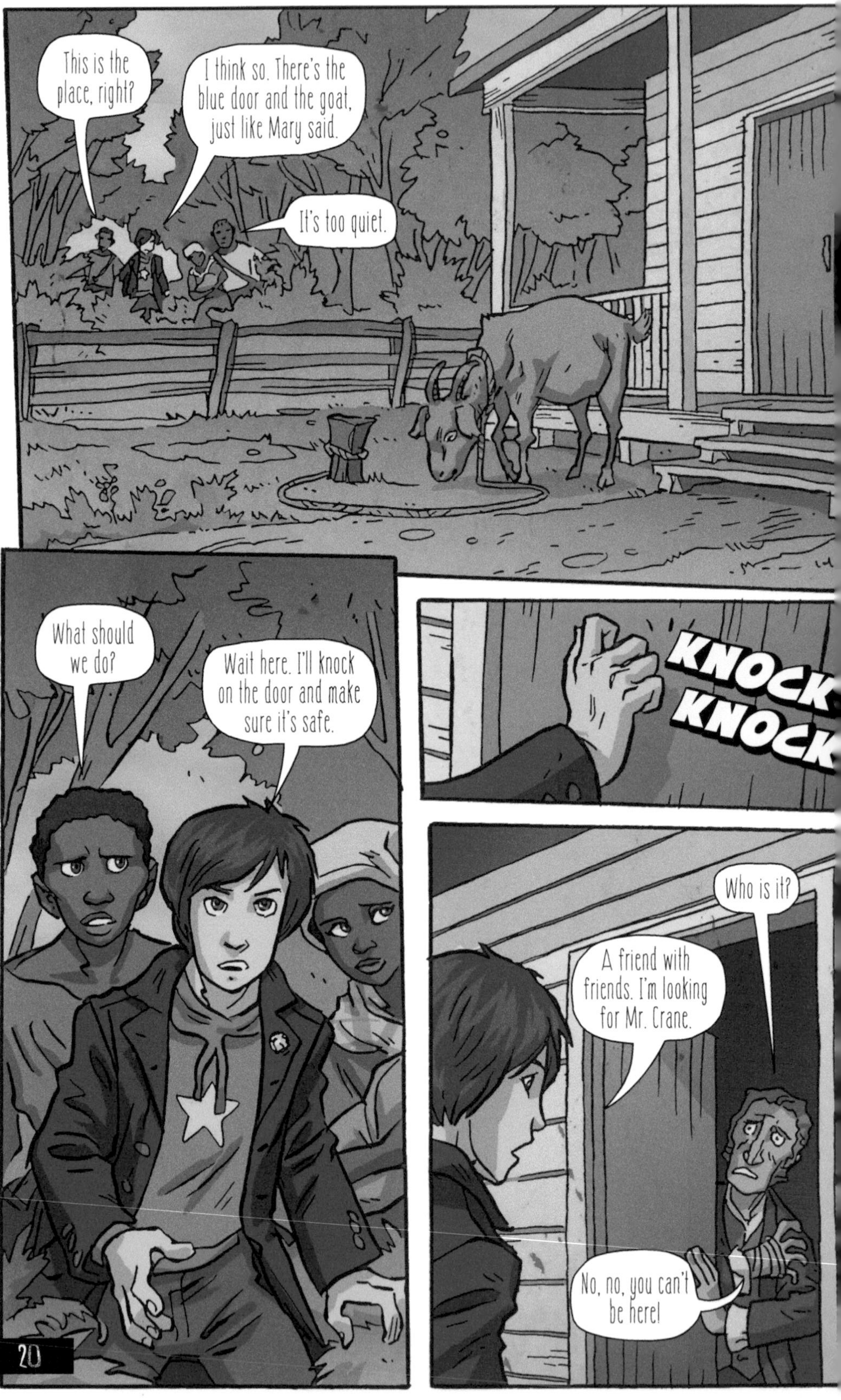
This is the place, right?
I think so. There's the blue door and the goat, just like Mary said.
It's too quiet.
What should we do?
Wait here. I'll knock on the door and make sure it's safe.
KNOCK KNOCK
Who is it?
A friend with friends. I'm looking for Mr. Crane.
No, no, you can't be here!

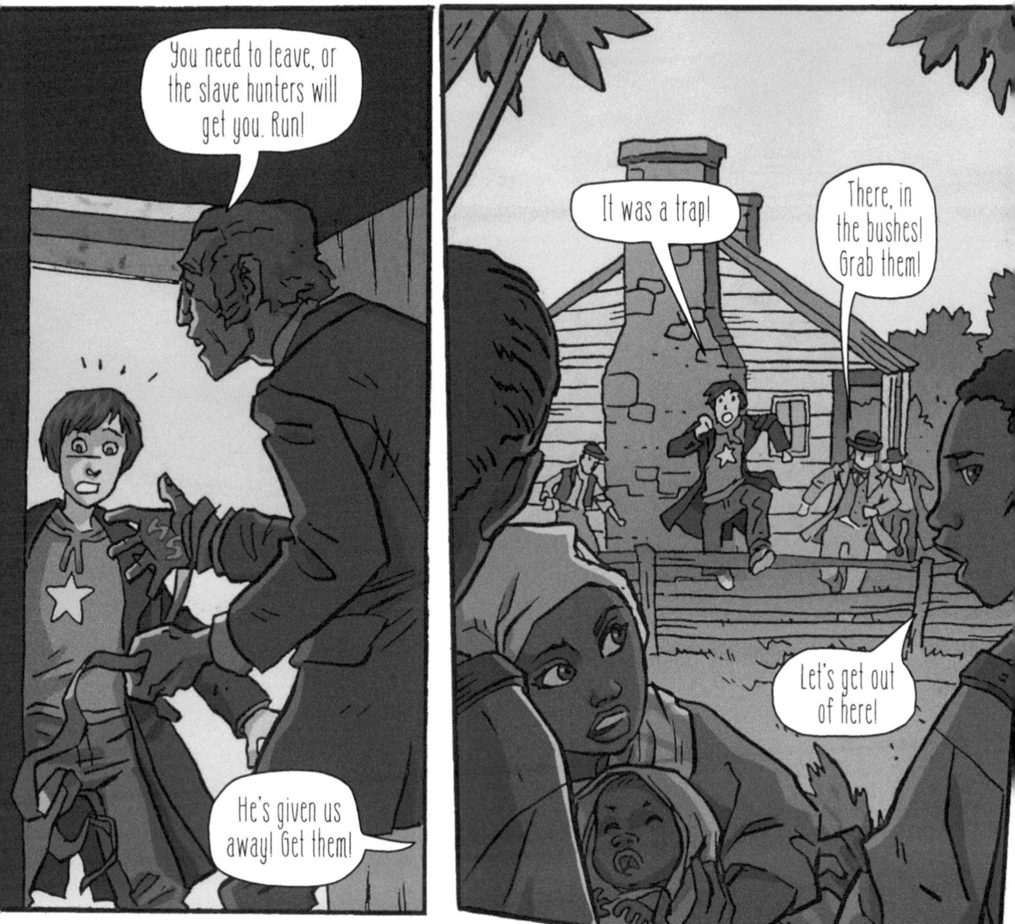
You need to leave, or the slave hunters will get you. Run!
He's given us away! Get them!
It was a trap!
There, in the bushes! Grab them!
Let's get out of here!
Chase down the family! They can't get far carrying a baby! We'll catch William later!

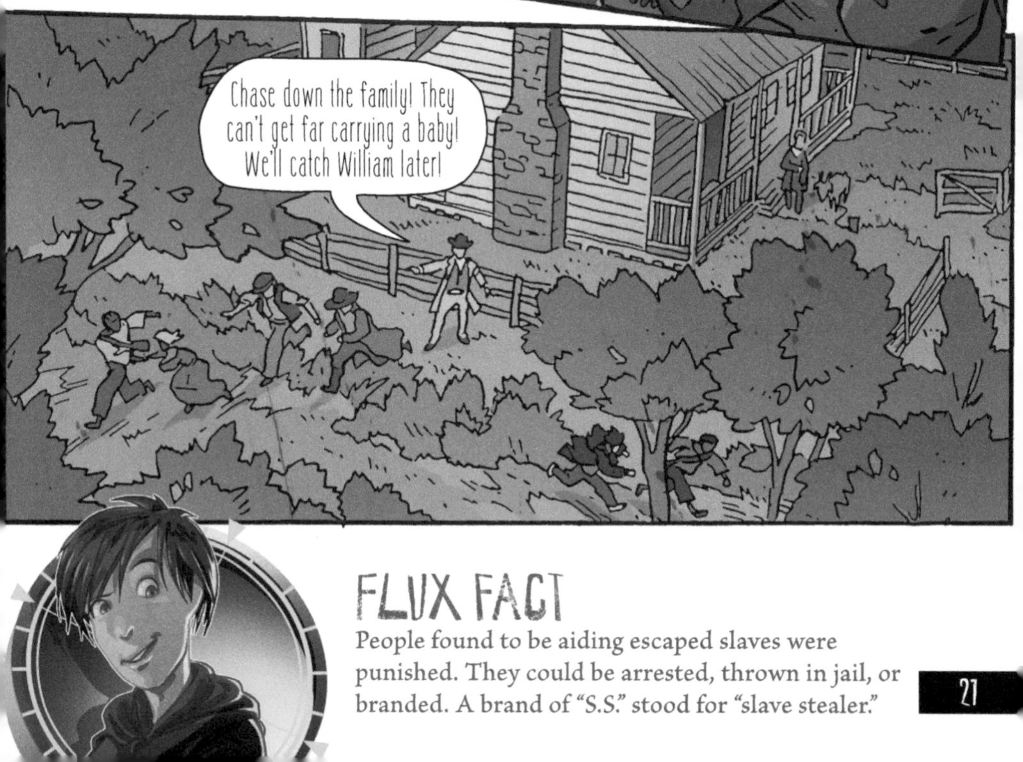

FLUX FACT

People found to be aiding escaped slaves were punished. They could be arrested, thrown in jail, or branded. A brand of "S.S." stood for "slave stealer."

CHAPTER FOUR

ONE RIVER TO CROSS

Covington, Kentucky; later that day

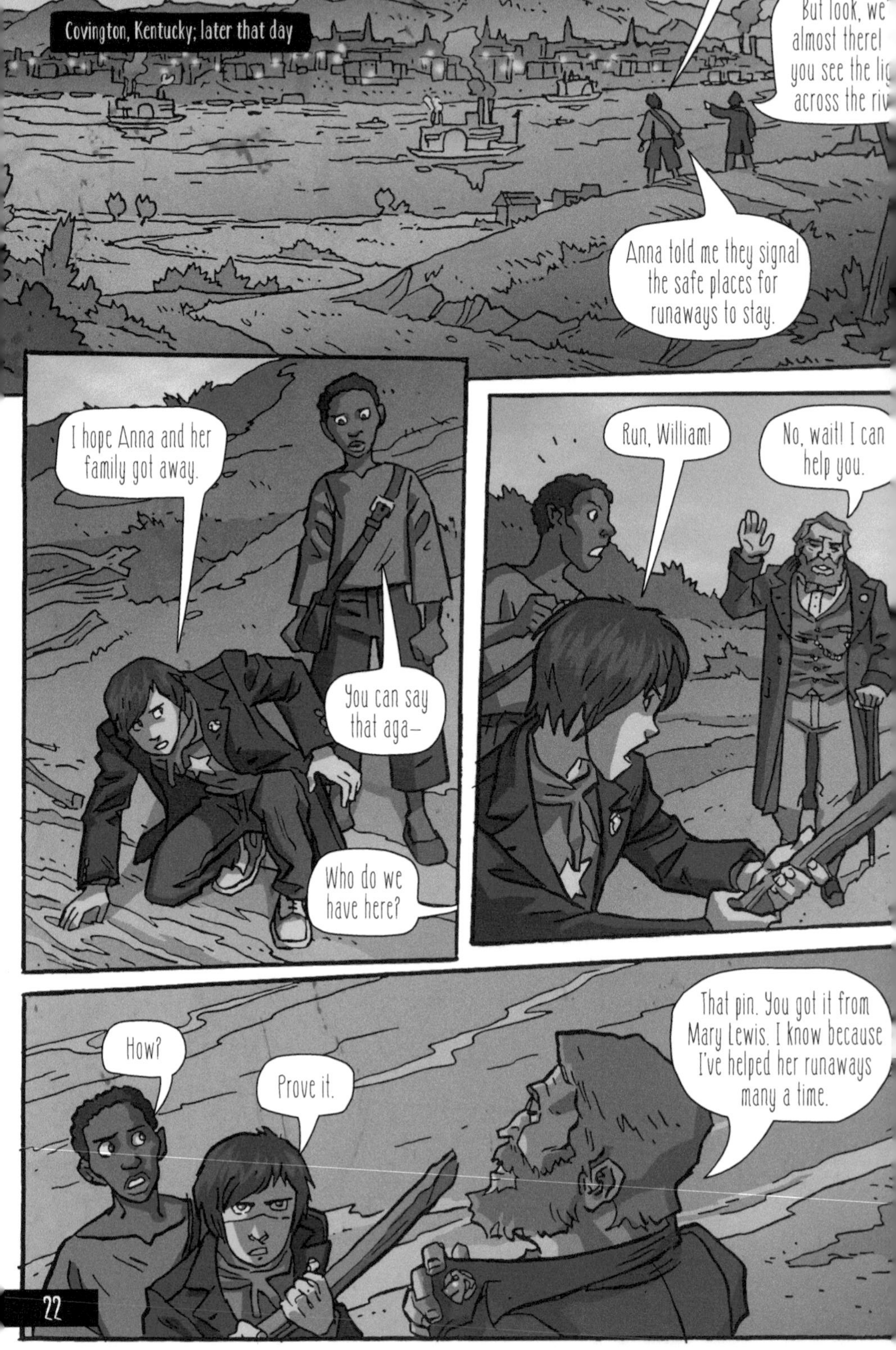
That was too close!
But look, we almost there! you see the li across the riv
Anna told me they signal the safe places for runaways to stay.
I hope Anna and her family got away.
You can say that aga—
Who do we have here?
Run, William!
No, wait! I can help you.
How?
Prove it.
That pin. You got it from Mary Lewis. I know because I've helped her runaways many a time.

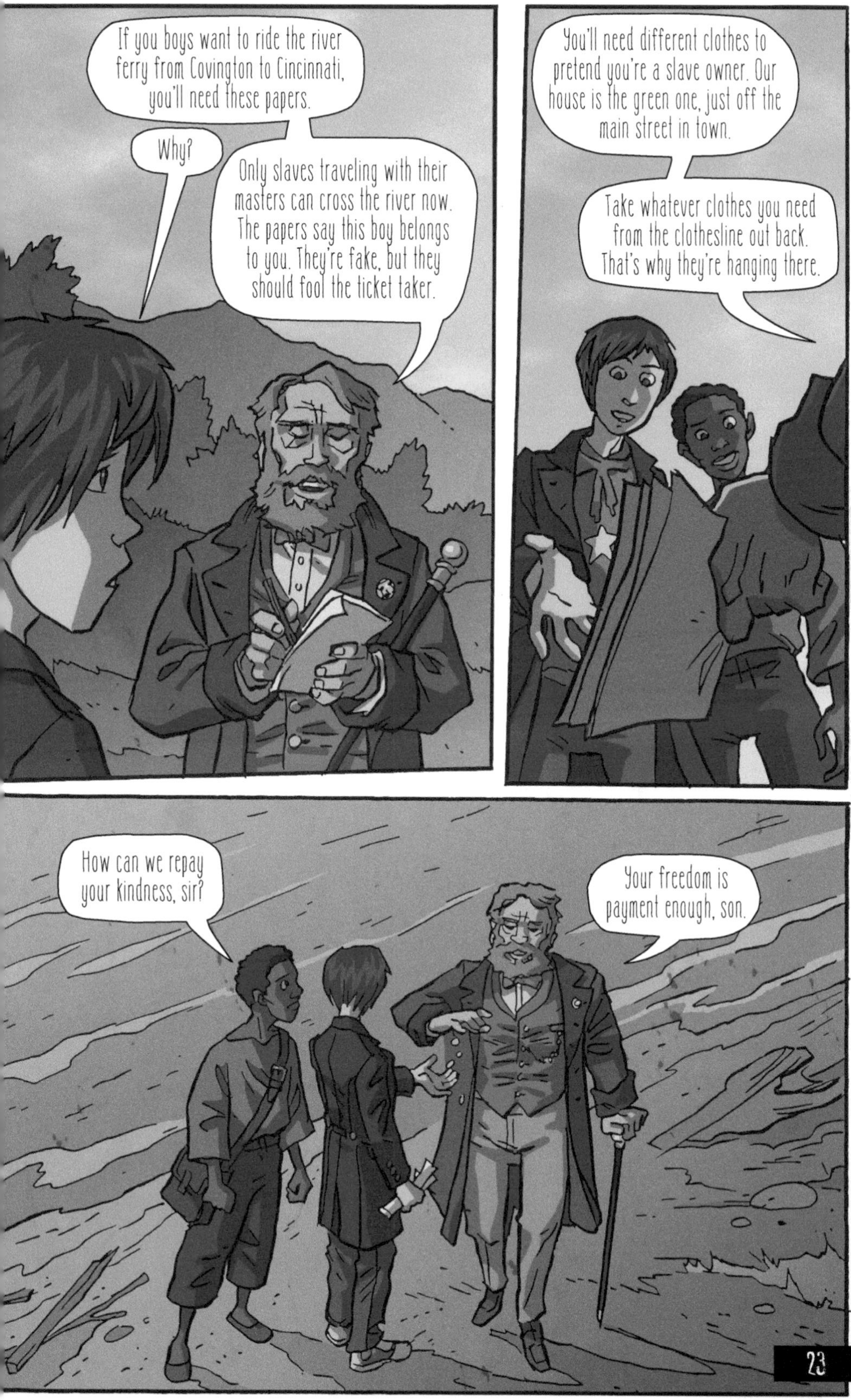
If you boys want to ride the river ferry from Covington to Cincinnati, you'll need these papers.
Why?
Only slaves traveling with their masters can cross the river now. The papers say this boy belongs to you. They're fake, but they should fool the ticket taker.
You'll need different clothes to pretend you're a slave owner. Our house is the green one, just off the main street in town.
Take whatever clothes you need from the clothesline out back. That's why they're hanging there.
How can we repay your kindness, sir?
Your freedom is payment enough, son.

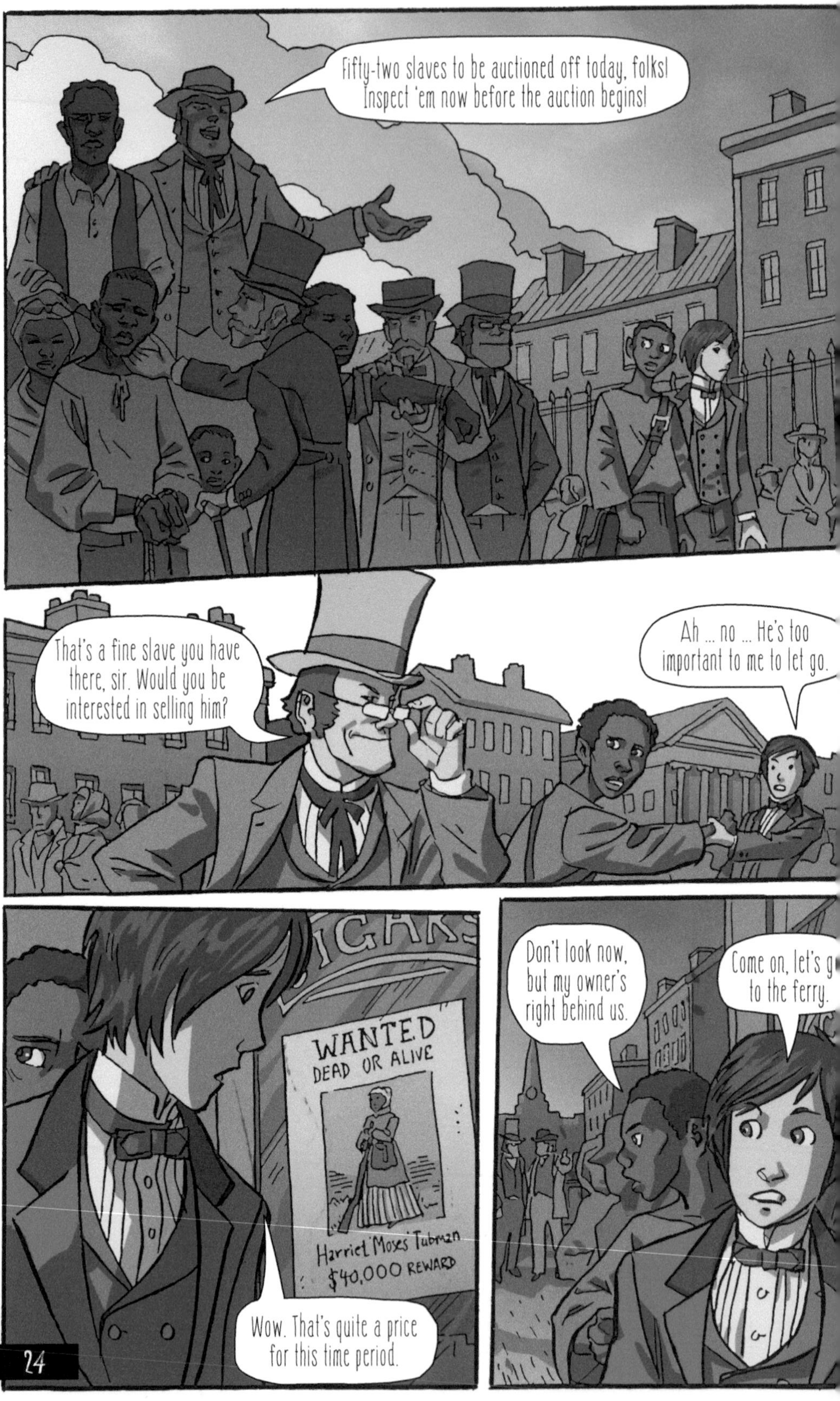
Fifty-two slaves to be auctioned off today, folks! Inspect 'em now before the auction begins!
That's a fine slave you have there, sir. Would you be interested in selling him?
Ah ... no ... He's too important to me to let go.
WANTED
DEAD OR ALIVE
Harriet 'Moses' Tubman
$40,000 REWARD
Wow. That's quite a price for this time period.
Don't look now, but my owner's right behind us.
Come on, let's g
to the ferry.

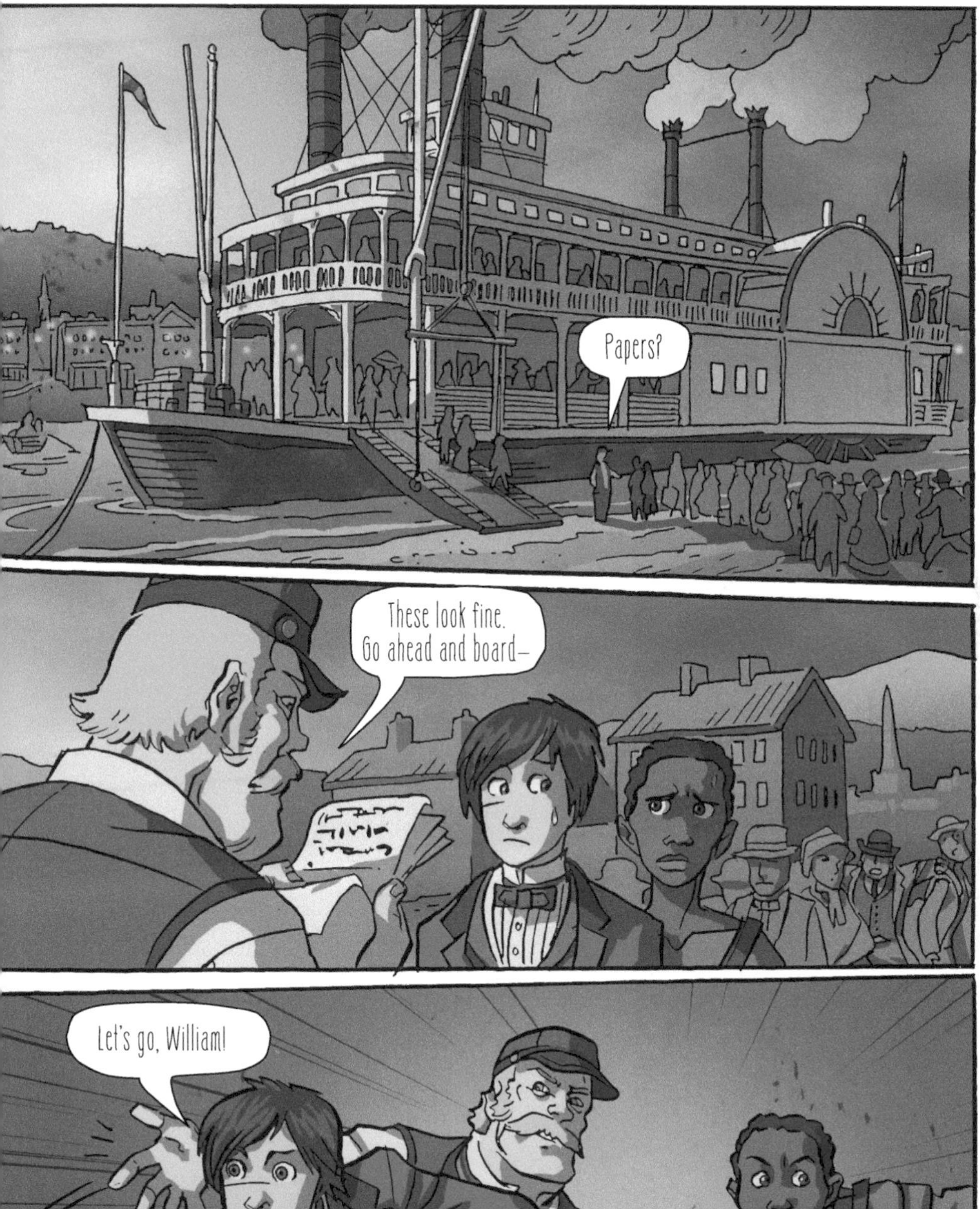
Papers?
These look fine. Go ahead and board–
Let's go, William!

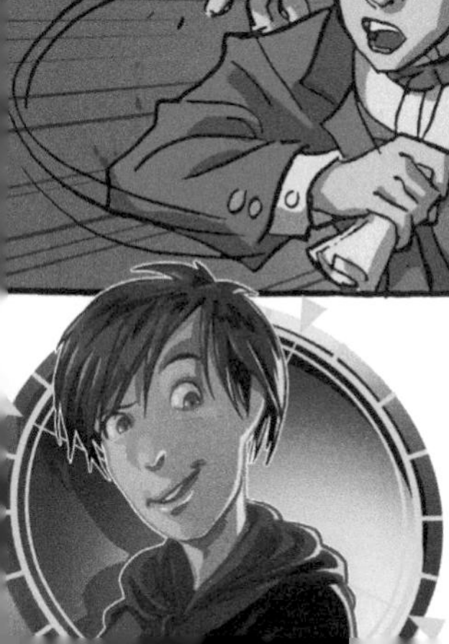

FLUX FACT

Former slave Harriet "Moses" Tubman made 19 trips into the South in 10 years. She brought more than 300 slaves to freedom. Her nickname, "Moses," came from the Bible prophet who led his people to freedom.

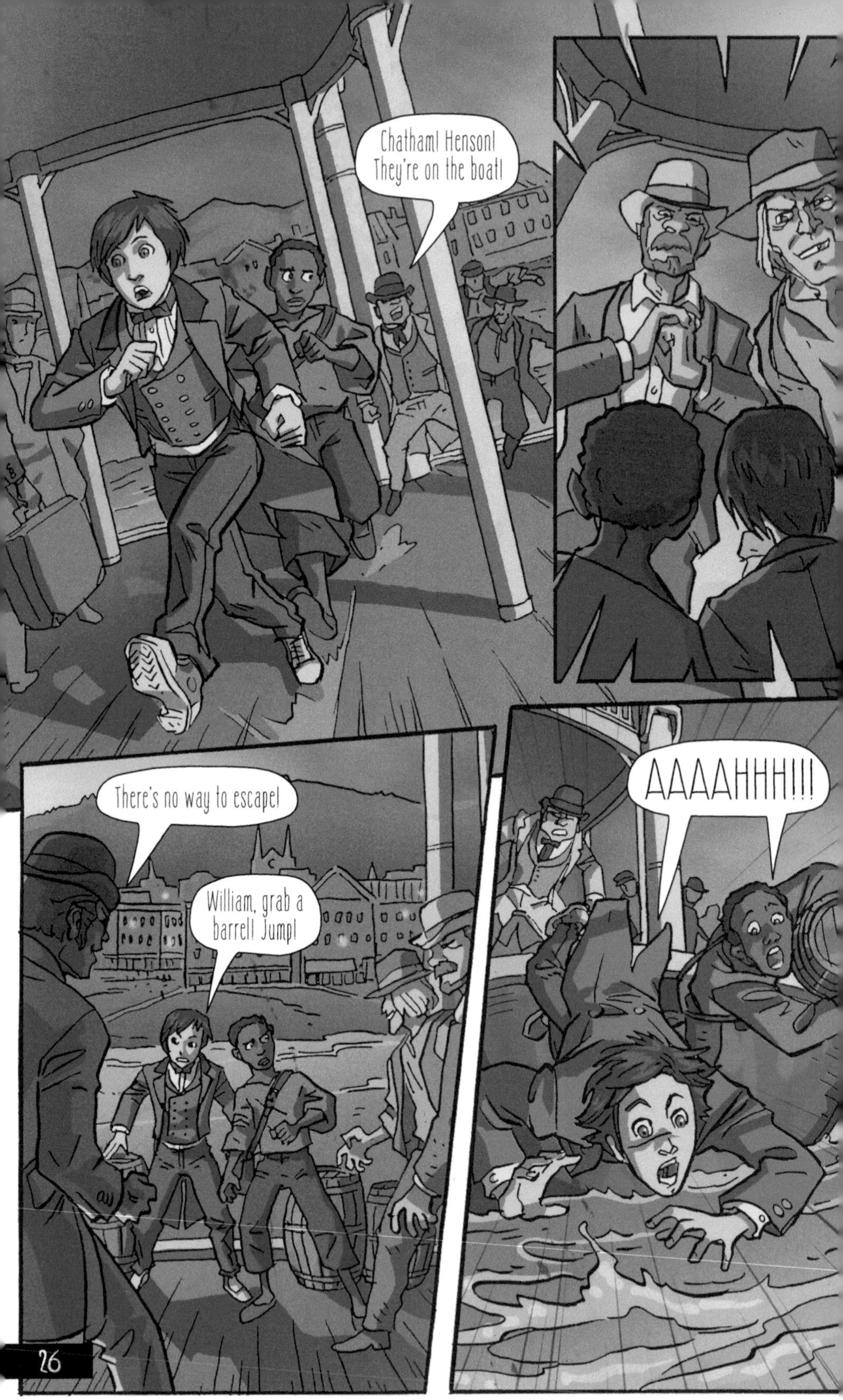
Chatham! Henson! They're on the boat!
There's no way to escape!
William, grab a barrel! Jump!
AAAAHHH!!!

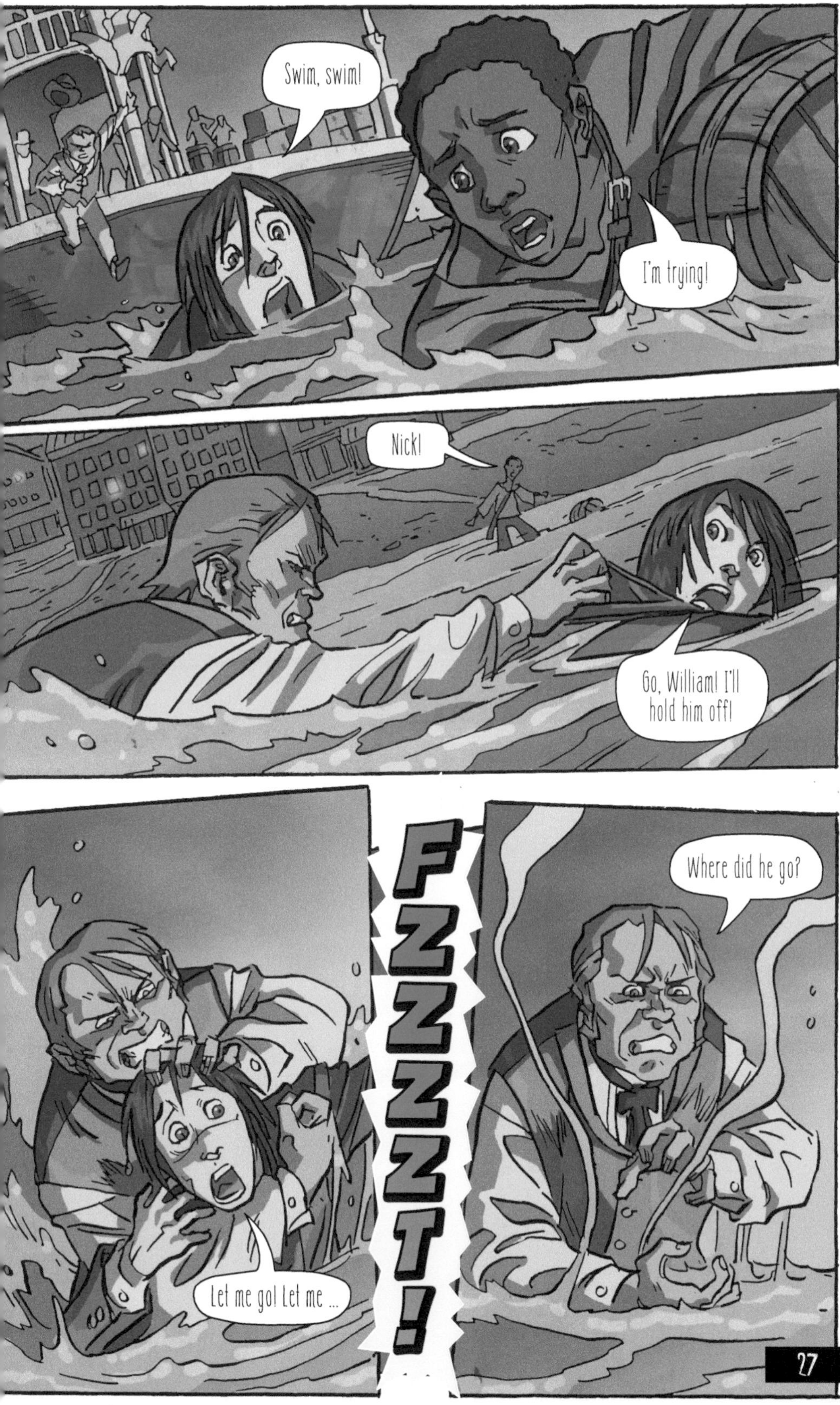
Swim, swim!
I'm trying!
Nick!
Go, William! I'll hold him off!
Let me go! Let me ...
FZZZZT!
Where did he go?

CHAPTER FIVE

FINDING FREEDOM

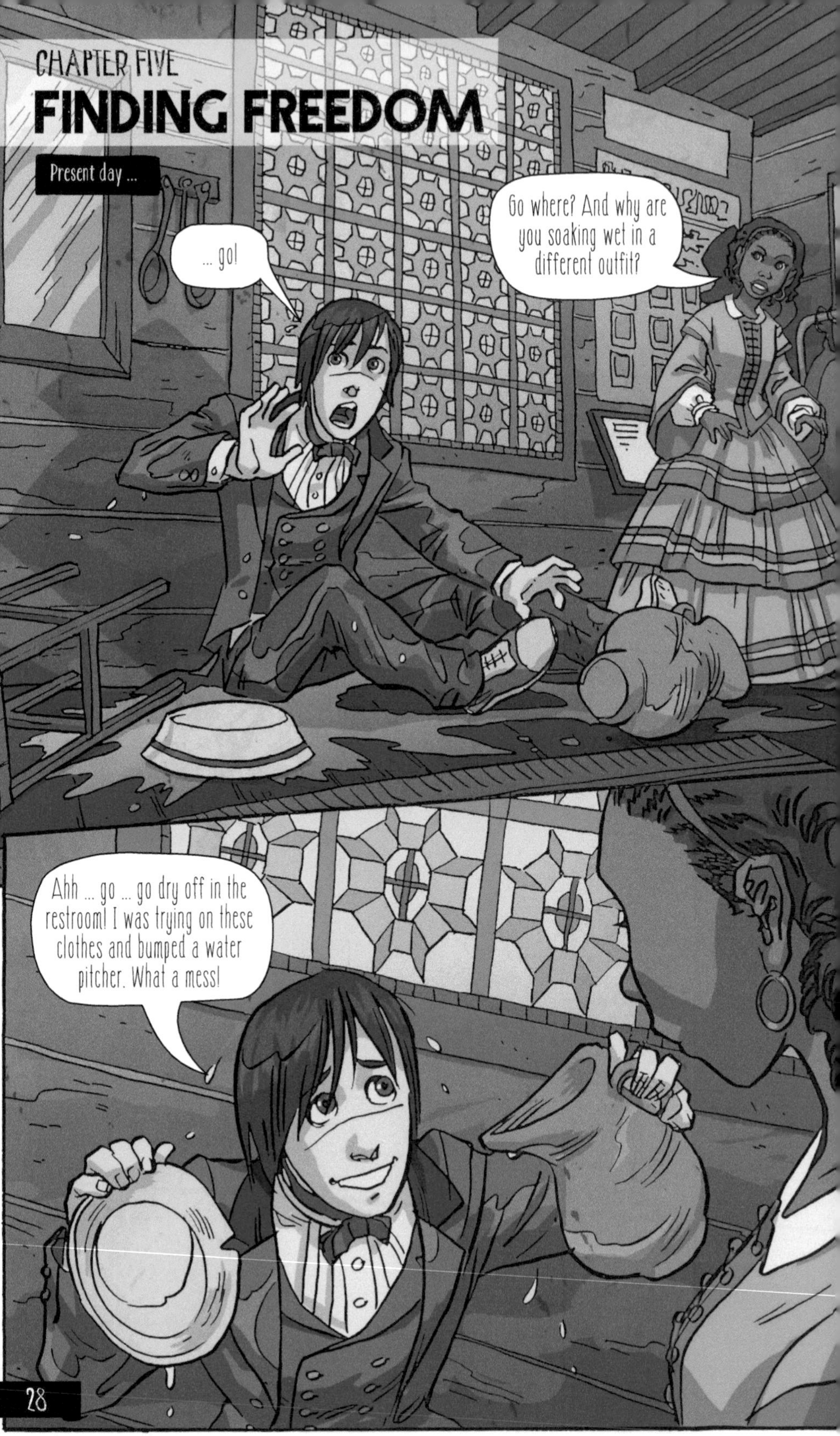
Present day ...
... go!
Go where? And why are you soaking wet in a different outfit?
Ahh ... go ... go dry off in the restroom! I was trying on these clothes and bumped a water pitcher. What a mess!

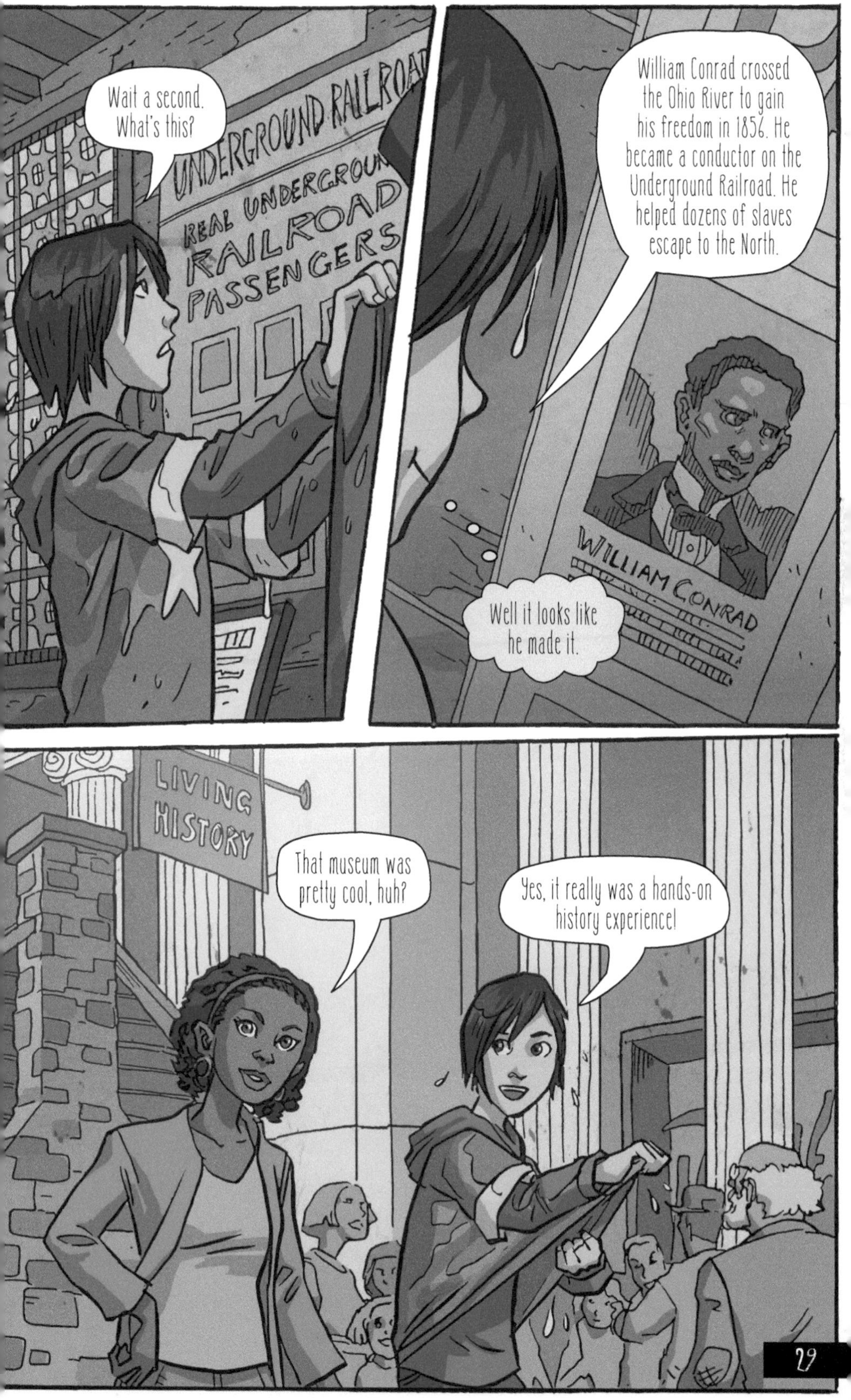
Wait a second. What's this?
RAILROAD PASSENGERS
William Conrad crossed the Ohio River to gain his freedom in 1856. He became a conductor on the Underground Railroad. He helped dozens of slaves escape to the North.
WILLIAM CONRAD
Well it looks like he made it.
LIVING HISTORY
That museum was pretty cool, huh?
Yes, it really was a hands-on history experience!

FLUX FILES

THE FIRST SLAVES

The first slaves arrived in Virginia in 1619. By 1790 nearly 20 percent of the 3.9 million people living in the United States were slaves.

THE COTTON GIN

The African slave trade began to decline by the Revolutionary War (1775–1783). However, the invention of the cotton gin in 1793 changed things. This machine quickly separated cotton fibers from cotton seeds. Cotton became the main crop grown in the South. Plantation owners needed slaves to work the cotton fields.

SMUGGLING SLAVES

The African slave trade was banned in 1808. However, slaves were still smuggled into the country. And those already in the country—and the children they had—were still kept as slaves.

RAILROAD ORIGINS

The Underground Railroad first began in the mid-1810s. It became more organized in the late 1830s when a man named Robert Purvis formed an organization to help runaway slaves. People who helped slaves escape started to think of the safe houses as stations, or stops, on a railroad line.

NAMING THE RAILROAD

Legend says that the Underground Railroad got its name in 1831. That year a slave named Tice Davids crossed the Ohio River. His owner was not far behind. When Davids reached the Ohio shore, he disappeared. His master told people that Davids must have escaped on an "underground railroad."

FAMOUS CONDUCTORS

Conductors on the Underground Railroad helped thousands of slaves escape to freedom. Robert Purvis and Levi Still helped at least 9,000 slaves each. Levi Coffin and Thomas Garrett aided another 6,000 total. John Rankin and his family helped around 2,000 escapees.

TENSION OVER SLAVERY

Disagreements over slavery created tension between northern and southern states. In 1860 South Carolina became the first southern state to secede from the Union. Ten other states would later secede as well. These states formed the Confederate States of America. The war between the Union and the Confederate States became known as the Civil War (1861–1865).

FREEDOM

In 1862 the Union announced that any black men who enlisted during the Civil War would be given certificates of freedom. The next year President Abraham Lincoln released the Emancipation Proclamation. This document granted freedom to all slaves in Confederate territory. The 13th Amendment abolished slavery in the United States in 1865.

GLOSSARY

ABOLISH (uh-BOL-ish)—to put an end to something

AUCTION (AWK-shuhn)—a sale during which items are sold to the person who offers the most money

BRAND (BRAND)—to mark the skin with a hot iron, sometimes as a mark of disgrace

CONDUCTOR (kuhn-DUK-tuhr)—a person who helped runaway slaves escape to the North on the Underground Railroad

DETAIN (di-TAYN)—to hold someone back when he or she wants to go

EMANCIPATION (i-MAN-si-pay-shuhn)—freedom from slavery or control

FUGITIVE (FYOO-juh-tiv)—someone who is running from the law

PILOT (PYE-luht)—a person who traveled into slave states to find slaves who were seeking freedom

PLANTATION (plan-TAY-shuhn)—a large farm where crops such as cotton and sugarcane are grown; before 1865 plantations were run by slave labor

PROPERTY (PROP-ur-tee)—a physical object that belongs to someone

PROPHET (PROF-it)—a person who claims to be a messenger of God

SECEDE (si-SEED)—to formally withdraw from a group or an organization, often to form another organization

READ MORE

BAUMANN, SUSAN K. *Harriet Tubman: Conductor of the Underground Railroad.* Jr. Graphic African-American History. New York: PowerKids Press, 2014.

MCDONOUGH, YONA ZELDIS. *What Was The Underground Railroad? What Was …?* New York: Grosset & Dunlap, 2013.

WHELAN, GLORIA, AND GWENYTH SWAIN. *Voices for Freedom.* American Adventures. Ann Arbor, Mich.: Sleeping Bear Press, 2013.

INTERNET SITES

FactHound offers a safe, fun way to find Internet sites related to this book. All sites on FactHound have been researched by our staff.

Here's all you do:

Visit *www.facthound.com*

Type in this code: 9781491402542

Super-cool stuff!

Check out projects, games and lots more at
www.capstonekids.com

INDEX

ABOUT THE AUTHOR

Mari Bolte is an author of children's books and a lover of history. A degree in anthropology has given her an appreciation for other people in other times. She lives in southern Minnesota with her husband and daughter.

ALL OF NICKOLAS FLUX ADVENTURES

ARRESTED FOR WITCHCRAFT!
NICKOLAS FLUX
AND THE SALEM WITCH TRIALS

DEFEND UNTIL DEATH!
NICKOLAS FLUX
AND THE BATTLE OF THE ALAMO

Flight to FREEDOM!
NICKOLAS FLUX
AND THE UNDERGROUND RAILROAD

Night of Rebellion!
NICKOLAS FLUX
AND THE BOSTON TEA PARTY

PERIL IN POMPEII!
NICKOLAS FLUX
AND THE ERUPTION OF MOUNT VESUVIUS

STAKE A CLAIM!
NICKOLAS FLUX
AND THE CALIFORNIA GOLD RUSH

READ THEM ALL!

SURPRISE ATTACK!
NICKOLAS FLUX
AND THE ATTACK ON PEARL HARBOR

TRACKING AN ASSASSIN!
NICKOLAS FLUX
AND THE ASSASSINATION OF ABRAHAM LINCOLN

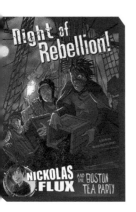

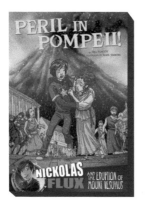

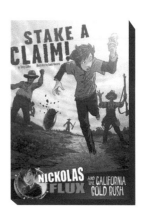